THE MORAL LIMITATIONS OF CAPITALISM

Other books by Irving S. Michelman:

Consumer Finance: A Case History in American Business
Business at Bay: Critics and Heretics of American Business
The Crisis Meeters: Business Response to Social Crises
The Roots of Capitalism in Western Civilization: A Socioeconomic
   Assessment

The Moral Limitations of Capitalism

IRVING S. MICHELMAN

Former corporate executive and advisor to Federal Reserve Board and US Department of Commerce.

Avebury

Aldershot • Brookfield USA • Hong Kong • Singapore • Sydney

Published by
Avebury
Ashgate Publishing Limited
Gower House
Croft Road
Aldershot
Hants GU11 3HR
England

Ashgate Publishing Company
Old Post Road
Brookfield
Vermont 05036
USA

British Library Cataloguing in Publication Data

Michelman, Irving S.
    Moral Limitations of Capitalism –
    (Avebury Series in Philosophy)
    I. Title II. Series
    330.122
ISBN 1 85628 877 3

Reprinted 1996

Library of Congress Cataloging-in-Publication Data

Michelman, Irving S.
    The moral limitations of capitalism / Irving S. Michelman.
        p. cm. – (Avebury series in philosophy)
    Includes index.
    ISBN 1-85628-877-3 : $59.95 (est.)
    1. Capitalism–Moral and ethical aspects. 2. Distributive justice.
    3. Capitalism–United States–Case studies. I. Title. II. Series.
    HB501.M632 1994
    174'.4–dc20
                                                          94-22129
                                                          CIP

Typeset by Breeze Limited, Manchester.

Printed in Great Britain by Ipswich Book Co. Ltd., Ipswich,

For Shirley

Contents

Acknowledgments

I would like to express warm thanks to Robert Heilbroner for his steady encouragement and valuable suggestions. Others in the academic field who were extremely gracious and helpful are Russell Hardin of University of Chicago and New York University, Seymour Drescher of University of Pittsburgh, John Patrick Diggins of CUNY, James MacGregor Burns of Williams College, Martha Nussbaum of Brown University, Stuart Hampshire, eminent British moral philosopher, and Frank Michelman and Archibald Cox of Harvard University Law School. I am also grateful to Federal Judge Richard A. Posner, US Court of Appeals, Chicago, and Archbishop Rembert G. Weakland, OSB, Milwaukee.

I also thank David Lamb of University of Manchester, Editor of the Avebury Series in Philosophy, who recognized my book as a venture in moral philosophy as well as in economics. My thanks also to Anita Goswami for preparation of the manuscript. My easiest decision is to express thanks to my wife.

Introduction

This book seeks a moral measurement for democratic capitalism to supplement its cornucopia of goods and services. The search is encouraged by capitalism's record as an institution receptive to continuing and successful reform. It is fortified by evidence that capitalism, like democracy, eventually responds to the urgency of changed social expectations. It claims that capitalism, immensely powerful, has met its match in modern pluralist democracy.

There is also the assumption in this book that laissez-faire capitalism has seen its day in America, despite tendencies to represent it as reality rather than memory. Finally, while benign capitalists are all to the good, and should be well-rewarded, the three branches of government, and the mediating institutions of press, church, and the intellectual establishment, are indispensable moderators for such a pervasive system. A personal judgment rounds out this overview: the forces of capitalism recognize their bounty, and willingly trade off government welfarism as a form of ransom for the inequalities and privileges inherent in the system. There are now 500,000 millionaires in America enduring regulated capitalism.[1]

* * *

Historically, the major reforms imposed on business institutions in the twentieth century have concentrated on restricting the raw power of capitalism, the first economic system to enjoy relative autonomy from the reigning political system. Moral measurement has not been a priority in establishing the power equilibrium between the state and modern capitalism. As ultimate countervailing authority, the state entered the regulatory arena reluctantly, largely because of the breakdown of the economy during the Great Depression. Capitalism, by its nature preoccupied with profits, has neither Utopian nor moral ambitions. Its legitimacy has rested on unprecedented material deliveries in peace and war, and a hard-earned compatibility with democracy. Democracy has been preoccupied with securing the negative civil rights related to political abuse. It is now time to propose positive economic rights for democracy's intractable, least-advantaged citizens. Here is where the moral measurement for capitalism should start. The new criteria for rights to be proposed in this book are first, more fairness in distribution of economic resources; and second, the dignity and security arising from the ability to work gainfully during one's lifetime work span.

Additionally, this book differs from traditional analysis by introducing a strong element of moral philosophy. Moral philosophers, especially those concerned with social justice, inevitably shape and moderate our political and economic systems. Operating in the realm of principles and values, their proposals are long-term in effect, but generally moral ideas precede fundamental economic change, some with baleful, others with benign, results. Aristotle, St. Thomas Aquinas, Adam Smith, Rousseau, Karl Marx, and John Rawls are among those called upon under this proviso. They help us understand capitalism before we evaluate it.

* * *

Morality being suspect, often with good reason, this book approaches the subject circumspectly by introducing first a conservative, efficiency model of capitalism claiming moral credentials. It then presents three moral analogues, in preparation for the moral-measurement encounter. It does so in the belief that observing capitalism from other perspectives than its function in the marketplace is good preparation for prescribing principles of economic justice.

The three moral analogues are intended to hold a mirror to capitalism's claim for legitimacy, meaning the moral as well as practical justification enjoyed by democracy.

xii

The first analogue examines in depth the 'virtues' concept in moral philosophy. This concept is the most enduring model for 'just' personal and public standards to be found in western civilization. The virtues hardly qualify as a political campaign banner, but how we live our lives and what we expect from our public institutions should matter most, if we claim to occupy moral ground.

The second analogue relates to capitalism's startlingly ambiguous experience with slavery, America's – and England's – most searing moral failure, yet redemptive for capitalism.

The third analogue reviews the Supreme Court's encounter with capitalism, illustrating through the Court's economic cases how a government institution moderated democratic capitalism and helped prepare it for the twenty-first century. The book concludes by analyzing two views on the future of capitalism, and by proposing some principles for capitalism's ongoing success.

Why use such analogues rather than traditional history and chronology? The plan of this book is basically to heighten our moral consciousness about the role of capitalism by viewing it largely from non-market, institutional perspectives. The analogue is a time-honored variation of the parable and the allegory. Its narrative feature provides an emotional content that complements the essentially rational point of view of both moral philosophy and traditional economics. There are certainly alternate routes for ruminating about the moral limitations of capitalism, but a predilection for analogy can be an advantage.

Notes

1 Information from the Joint Economic Committee of Congress, using data from a survey conducted by the University of Michigan. 420,000 families had net assets of at least $2.5 million. See *Wall Street Journal*, 28 July, 1986.

1 Judge Posner's Efficiency Theory for socially-just distribution

1 Some Ground Rules for Theory

We start with a theory about how the economic pie should be allocated. Not the theory of either super-rival, socialism or capitalism, but a garden variety within the capitalist system, entitled 'wealth-maximization' by its sponsor, Richard A. Posner. We need not be thrown off by the title. It is not a handbook for organized greed, nor a justification of anything so egoistically self-interested. It aligns itself with theories of justice, more particularly economic justice. As such, it is in the tradition of the founding father of capitalist theory, Adam Smith, who discerned benign, if not just, results from profit-seeking on the part of self-interested entrepreneurs, organized in that direction by the invisible hand of market forces. Capitalism still lacks a comprehensive theory and none will be found in this book. Instead I propose that modern capitalism requires more than economic growth and a cornucopia of products for its survival. Certainly the demise of socialism in the USSR and the Eastern bloc countries is cause for only limited self-congratulation. Capitalism should submit to moral scrutiny as well as marketplace performance. Concepts like legitimation, validation, and justification ought to apply to capitalism as a system as they do to democracy as a system. Such concepts, which in the long run generally precede political or economic action, occur first in the realm of ideas, or more specifically in the abstractions of theory, or in the rhetoric of ideology. This book will confine itself essentially to matters relating to economic justice and thus to questions about capitalism. In 'wealth-maximization' we have such an introductory theory.

1

The basic procedural method used by Posner in developing his theory is economic analysis. As an example of how economic analysis produces wealth-maximizing results, Posner offers the choice of a 'negligence' system as against a 'strict liability' system in the provision of drivers' insurance. His choice, expressly hypothetical, is unlikely to emerge in the departments of state-regulated insurance, troubled though the regulators are with severe loss ratios, but the ideas involved are substantial.

The excessive loss ratios result primarily from our national talent for auto theft, insurance fraud, litigiousness, redlining (discrimination based on residence), alcoholism, and recurrent citizen demands for across-the-board rate reductions. All such costs – even the redlining can end as cost although intended as economizer – are considered 'externalities' in the language of theory construction. They are generally excluded provisionally in order to test theories against each other under basic, uncomplicated conditions. In matters of economic transactions, the stipulated ideal conditions are usually free markets, low transaction costs, no coercion, and adequate information. Even the last-named might require further stipulation. For example, when does the right to privacy in economic matters, such as tax compliance, or business competition, become more fundamental than the right to information? In such cases, the stipulated information might be reduced.[1] One can understand why theorists employ reductive analysis, preferring a level playing field for advancing their own structures while rejecting alternative theories.

The commonality of externalities among competing economic systems, incidentally, is a useful antidote against excessively ethical or moralistic comparisons. Capitalism is prolific in producing executive class demons, as Wall Street and Washington scandals demonstrate. The USSR, long before its claims of distributive moral superiority vanished in the breakdown of distribution itself, had its own representatives in high places, sons-in-law of the party elite, millionaire black marketeers, and major bureaucratic embezzlers, not just the hooligans of the daily press. The major distinctions lie beyond personal behavior, both in theory and in practice. In a democracy, moral conduct in citizens, like public virtue in politicians, though highly desirable, becomes essentially a matter of its own reward.

There are exceptions to consider, where private and public concerns converge, such as the personal responsibility of those in society's 'welfare net' to help themselves emerge, or of politicians to avoid humiliation and censure. This still leaves the heavy responsibility on institutions in relation to distributive justice, the subject of this book.

2 Coase's Efficient Bargaining Contribution

Back to Posner and his driver system choice of 'negligence' over a 'strict liability' system. Though impracticable, it is still more relevant than prior economic analysis candidates such as the ground-breaking Coase theorem (1960).[2] This analysis is typically related in terms of Coase's wheat farmers who failed to fence their farms properly against grazing cattlemen and for their pennypinching were asserted by Coase to have diminished their claims for compensation as victims. In fact, in a flash of insight often referred to as genius, Coase failed to see the wheat farmers as victims in the first place. Instead of following the usual moral intuition one naturally senses between invader and invaded, that the victim is easily identifiable, Coase postulated that, for efficiency's sake, in matters that can be economically settled (which would generally be all tort cases but not criminal ones), the concept of victim had best be forgotten. There are no victims.

The Coase theorem provides a method for settlement for the wheat farmers based on the concept of efficient bargaining. In this hypothetical concept, the familiar stipulations excluding externalities are made at the outset. It is assumed farmers and cattlemen are able to bargain freely, without transaction costs or other outside interference. Since neither party is a victim, and therefore neither has rights, as victim or otherwise, it makes no difference which party starts out to strike the bargain or must be satisfied. Either way it will end in some kind of equilibrium involving negotiated choices such as the cost of fences for either or both sides, or the limiting of the size of the cattle herd or the fields of wheat, in order to contain future damage. Finally, to insure that the total costs of satisfactory bargaining come to rest at the most efficient, and theoretically least expensive, point on an economic analysis scale, Coase prescribes that the bargain must

3

conform to an efficiency standard, the 'Pareto-superiority' criterion, described later in this chapter.

It was the objective of Coase, as of Posner, to keep all compensation and costs at a minimum, in the name of efficiency and whatever social goal it could lead to, such as Posner's wealth-maximizing. Coase is readily criticized for his unconditional neutrality, with its overtones of insensitivity regarding intuitions of right and wrong, indeterminate legal rights, and the concept of no victims. Excessive neutrality, or detachment from the human condition, is a risk which economic analysis inevitably faces, from Karl Marx's theory of economic determinism for an entire culture to Posner's wealth-maximizing, with varying degrees of success. A sophisticated critic might place exaggerated or emotional concerns on hold, while concentrating on the main thrust of the argument. For example, Charles Fried, Harvard law professor and philosopher, a rare Kantian moral autonomist in a world of utilitarian consequentialists, strongly devoted to rights and certain to whom they belong, still finds considerable merit in Coase's achievement. Coase's reversal of our commonplace, intuitive judgments challenges us 'to explain why not only our land is ours, our automobiles, but why our teeth, blood, kidneys, ideas and labor are our own.'[3] Further, adds Fried, it forces us to justify ethically why we claim such ownership, if they are credibly subject to such a challenge. It was an additional Coase contribution to advance the idea that the economizing of social costs, that is, their economic analysis, had been unconsciously followed by the English courts in deciding certain common law nuisance cases over the centuries, thus giving economic analysis imposing common law credentials, which Posner has since greatly enlarged.

I said above Posner's version was the more relevant for two reasons. First, the protection from harm or the right to compensation for it, in a society where autos impinge on our consciousness more than any other artifact and threaten us accordingly, merits radical analysis. We can visualize ourselves as drivers more readily than wheat farmers or cattlemen. Second, Posner, unlike his morally neutral conservative colleagues, notably Milton Friedman, assumes the role of moral philosopher as well as economic analyst in advancing his theory of wealth-maximization. In this role, he labors to justify his choices

4

morally by claiming they are consistent with Kantian principles of individual autonomy, evidenced through the medium of consent.

Keeping Coase's pioneering analysis in mind, under Posner's 'negligence' system, only where a driver is at fault (carelessly negligent) will he be held responsible for compensation to the injured person. Where neither party is at fault – 'the unavoidable accident' that so frequently appears – then Posner would not want either side liable to the other, as they are under customary 'strict liability' systems. In such cases there would be no compensation. (The Posner proposal should not be identified with 'no-fault' insurance operative in some states. This is a different matter, the same 'strict liability' but with the costly legal contest to determine who was at fault eliminated.)

How then would the victim be compensated? After all, he suffered injury through no fault of his own in a common activity of constant risk and necessity. A distinguished predecessor, Judge Learned Hand, made an explicit attempt at formulating the compensation involved in damage cases as early as 1940, a major instance of economic analysis applied in a high court setting.[4] (This in turn should be separated from what may be termed 'socioeconomic' considerations at a high court level, for example, those enlisted by Justice Holmes, by nature a conservative, to convince his associates, regardless of their economic prejudices, to accept the dominant 'felt necessities of the time,' such as a reasonable work week and the right to unionize, and to overrule or sustain state legislatures accordingly.)

Under the Hand formula, it is proposed that you have negligence, and are thus subject to compensation claims, when 'the burden of precautions' (costs of preventive care) that you may or may not have taken, were less than the probability of accident occurrence multiplied by the dollar loss should said accident occur (cost of losses). In other words, only to the extent you have underinsured or underprotected yourself against the contingency are you economically liable.

The Hand formula has limited application, particularly for auto accidents with their wide range of probabilities and potential costs of personal injuries. It is also, as one would expect from a judicial formula, notably absent in moral or ethical claims, other than the mathematics of the equation, which indicate equal consideration. The forthright economic formula is presented as rational on its face but not necessarily

5

morally grounded in any special way. Moral philosophers live or perish by validation of their theories, and Posner, respectful of Hand's ground-breaking, moves on to economic analysis validated by consent. His objective is to make wealth-maximizing ethically compelling.

3 Adding the Moral Dimension of Consent

Posner's doctrine of consent is derived from the efficiency principle of Vilfredo Pareto (1848–1923), the Italian economist and sociologist. Pareto's aim was to establish an ethical principle for the allocation of resources in general. It is another entry in the search for moral creden-tials for capitalism beginning with Adam Smith, sometime Professor of Moral Theology at the University of Glasgow, and author of *The Theory of Moral Sentiments*, (1759), as well as *The Wealth of Nations*, (1776).

Pareto's interest in establishing a revised efficiency principle was primarily to refute a perennial criticism (inability to establish personal preferences) of the dominant social policy construct of modern times, the utilitarian moral theory associated with Jeremy Bentham and John Stuart Mill. This theory, which swept the field among England's nine-teenth-century 'liberal' capitalists and politicians, continued to promote Adam Smith's restraints on state interference at both personal and public levels. Additionally it articulated, in its original classical form, a highly developed social and moral theory devoted to the active pursuit of personal and public good consequences. The criterion for 'good', in brief terms, is the greatest 'utility' (meaning 'welfare') for the society involved. Early utilitarian literature, particularly Bentham's, refers to this criterion in terms of 'greatest pleasure' and 'least pain'. As with most enduring theories, its loyal interpreters have turned utilitarianism into a movement rather than a fixed text. Thus its predominant flaws, such as the 'pleasure-pain' terminology, or the threat of individualism being crushed under the weight of collective benefits, or the charge of ends justifying ruthless or paternalistic means, have been explained away or modified with reasonable success.[5] Most prominent philosophers concerned with distributive justice today acknowledge utilitarianism in their proposals. Posner, for example, is only 'less utilitarian' than normal and 'less Kantian' than normal by his own definition.[6]

When Jefferson graciously included the 'pursuit of happiness' in the *Declaration* as an inalienable right for eighteenth-century architects of a new order, he may well have had in mind Bentham's original pleasure concept.[7] The Constitution itself is a political document with little economic message other than the federal government's concern for the general welfare. Additionally the Fifth and Fourteenth Amendments replace Jefferson's happiness concept with a more material and measureable objective. They specify that neither the federal government (the Fifth Amendment) nor the States (the Fourteenth Amendment) may 'deprive any person of life, liberty or *property* without due process of law.' Capitalism, of course, does not seek shelter in a written constitution. It is robustly non-theoretical, save for its generic roots in the market and profit systems, and to a considerable degree in prevailing power systems.[8] Still, in its commitment to Adam Smith's laissez-faire concept and to the notion of economic growth for mass improvement via productivity, or efficiency, capitalism is a natural ally of utilitarian social theory, as it is of political democracy.

Historically, the utilitarian concept of beneficent goals for large groups prevailed in modern industrial society because it worked. Like its counterpart in modern religion, the concept of the 'Protestant ethic', it harmonised with Adam Smith's vision of a constantly growing, efficient society producing goods at lower cost, enabling ever larger masses to enjoy a better standard of living. Utilitarian theory, like capitalism itself, faces the paradox that its original political impulse, the anti-state, anti-mercantilist, free-market mechanism so rigorously promoted by Smith and his followers centuries ago, is outdated in its classical form. Modern American capitalism, essentially pragmatic, has responded to an urbanized, mass-production, dependent labor society by making an accommodation with 'welfare' concepts, largely emanating from the ideological revolution on the Continent it left behind. The alliance generally requires spending by government, at federal and local levels, for the benefit of both capitalists and other interests, such as the needy, on a scale that would scandalize Bentham and Mill. By such association, I claim that if we are capitalists, our theoretical moral roots are utilitarian.

7

Pareto did not live to see an application of utilitarianism consistent with his new ethical principle on a scale of magnitude beyond belief. Over 30 million Americans receive old-age pensions in the form of Social Security cash payments. The problem, more academic than real, that Pareto attempted to answer at the beginning of the century was the charge, in the name of individualism, that utilitarianism was somehow immoral, certainly inadequate, because of its inability to sort out personal preferences. The boundaries were too vague. How could you possibly offer public housing, say, in the 1920s, to a large bloc of citizens when some would rather live in cottages, others feared high-rises, still others preferred their old homes repaired, and so on? The objections seem deliberately obstructive, but moral philosophers, then as now opposed to utilitarianism, raised the banner of 'interpersonal preferences' when in fact a simpler fear, governmental paternalism, was often the issue. In 1935, Social Security became law, curiously satisfying a portion of the argument by the fact that money, like oil, is fungible, good anywhere and any time. The method of allocation, with all participants receiving proportionate benefits, and later, cost of living increases, also satisfied Pareto's criterion in good working order.

The 'Pareto-superiority' criterion is distant from historical capitalist notions such as innovation, or speed-up assemblies, or the current favorite, organized intelligence, which have been used to represent efficiency's claims in terms of technology. Instead it proposes a 'no-losers' situation in human terms. Pareto-superiority, as an efficiency standard, states that one allocation of resources will be considered superior (meaning ethically superior) to another if at least one person is better off under the first choice and no one is worse off. The Pareto ethical limitation, it should be noted, differs from contemporary notions of altruistic redistributions and transfer payments to the disadvantaged. It is primarily a commitment to strict but fair bargaining over resources among claimants, played on a stage of open information, without transaction costs and without consideration of third parties affected by the transaction. Still, a floor is placed under all economic transactions, preventing the bottom percentile from further downslide, through providing what later generations would call a 'welfare net' limitation. Conversely, if the top group wants more of society's resources, the whole ship of state, captain and cabin-boy alike, must float upward, not just the gross national product, for Pareto-superiority.

The water metaphor, though not Pareto's, surfaced again in the 1980s with the flowering of supply-side economic theory. It was used to symbolize the conservative concept that tax reduction on the part of a retreating central government would not only create greater product and wealth but would also carry upward the bottom percentile, through job creation, more effectively than billions in subsidies heretofore spent by an inefficient and presumably liberal bureaucracy. The '80s were distorted largely by massive Cold War expenditures, a reversal in trade balances, and the emergence of an immobile welfare population, so the effectiveness of supply-side theory, associated with enormous budget deficits and income class gaps, remains controversial. Note should be taken of its ethical ambitions, traceable to Pareto antecedents, however indirectly or vaguely conceived.

* * *

How does Posner derive consent from Pareto? As observers of theory, we might first consider the nature of his enterprise. Theory builders, however speculative, command our attention when the net result is an original contribution. Such contributions are rarely inspired; they all have roots and antecedents. In this case, Posner's original contribution is his concept of wealth-maximizing as an ethical social structure, attained by means of economic analysis, his acknowledged procedural domain. Because such contributions are syncretic or incremental, somewhat as in the development of religious doctrine, a pattern of synthesis is often involved in the theoretical enterprise.

Contemporary moral philosophy generally follows such a pattern. First, critical analysis of consequentialist theory, in the form of utilitarianism. Its dominance is challenged on grounds already noted, but also for its dependence on reason, the original keystone of western philosophy but currently in disfavor. The new favorite in the pattern is Aristotle, not consequentialist, but with a teleological, or goal-oriented theory of happiness arising from a life well-lived, conditioned along lines of self-perfection. (The reasons for the

Aristotelian revival will be discussed in Chapter 2.) As counterpoint, the analysis turns to deontological theories, where morality is a matter not primarily of results, nor of pursuit of excellence, but of obligation and duty, exemplified in the moral philosophy of Immanuel Kant, with his emphasis on autonomous and unconditional actions. Since the streams of theory are presented in their classical, or least persuasive, forms, they are more often than not evaluated as logically inconsistent, deficient on grounds of validation, or excessively dependent on reason. In short, the existing moral topography is found to be in need of renovation, which the new entrant is prepared to offer on some amended or improved basis.

One should show respect for these weighty efforts and not succumb to envy, itself a deadly sin. Still a good deal of current moral philosophy is spent on internecine aggression. Opponents are demolished, their principles are declared incoherent, self-contradictory, or beyond the limits of logical discourse. In a recent prominent work, an entire philosophic movement, the eighteenth-century Enlightenment, is pronounced a 'failure', terminating useful moral inquiry thereafter.[9]

I find this diversity of thought stimulating, appropriate for the marketplace of ideas that nourishes capitalism. There is also a recent development of parochial interest for capitalism. For decades, dominance in philosophic studies was maintained by the analytic school, which held that value judgments were basically off-limits. Since such judgments were at best relative, affected by personal emotions and attitudes, moral philosophers were urged to refrain from normative or prescriptive evaluations of what is right and wrong, to stay, like some good detective, with the facts, or with an analysis of the language in which the facts were presented, in order to reach a rational choice for action. The social sciences were similarly restrained by their peer leaders, with better reason, since they measure things more accurately than philosophers.[10] The philosophers nevertheless have been asking for prescriptive answers to how one should live, at least since Socrates questioned the unexamined life. Such contests about restraints on value judgments never end, swinging back and forth according to the ascendancy of either absolutism or relativism, the fundamental branches of philosophic thought. The first, absolutism, is at home with timeless value judgments, with what we ought to do; and the second,

10

relativism, is unsure it is safe to leave the modern haven of measure-able facts and observations.

Our field of inquiry is distributive justice and it is here that conventional theory has been breached in recent years, with the appearance of John Rawls's *A Theory of Justice*, in 1971, and Robert Nozick's *Anarchy, State and Utopia*, in 1974. In these widely noted books, Rawls's principles are moderately liberal and Nozick's uncompromisingly libertarian, but both are concerned with theories of economic distribution and involve value judgments. Neither of these works, which are often analyzed and used as points of departure by subsequent 'justice philosophers', including Posner, are endorsements of modern capitalism, much less in praise of it, in the tradition of F.A. Hayek or Milton Friedman. As philosophers, they are content to speculate quite abstractly about basic principles, away from the limitations of nation-states and the economic trade-offs taking place in their legislatures. Still, Rawls, Nozick and their successors offer a platform for the reflective measurement of capitalism, if not through a comprehensive theory, which capitalism by its pragmatic nature rightfully resists, then from the subsection of moral theory, where questions about fairness and validity in the distribution of resources can be asked.

Further, since most of the scholarly, and many of the best, analyses of capitalism (see your library microfiches) have received their impulse from Marx's prodigious imagination, these new entries make a distinct change from such supremacy. They are non-ideological in the sense of not being hostage to a master-intellect. But they also share, whether liberal or conservative, a similarity in values by assigning priority to underlying principles of liberty and freedom. Beyond these abstractions, both Rawls and Nozick claim the moral virtue of justice to justify their fundamental operating principles. In Rawls's case, a claim is made for just restraints on economic inequalities. In Nozick's, the overriding concern is the just inviolability of property ownership against all contending claims. It is my feeling that these distinguished opposing theorists, though they would strenuously decline the honor, given the bare choice between responsible capitalism and any other system, would become standard-bearers. With this prelude in mind, we turn now to expanding our moral capacity through exploration of three analogues: the virtues (personal and public behav-

11

ior), slavery (institutional failure and redemption), and constitutional law (institutional success), Chapters 2 through 6. This, of course, is the plan of the book, a wide-ranging alternative method intended to create awareness of theory and heightened moral consciousness about distribution of resources rather than cataloging the failure of communism and the triumph of capitalism.

, * * *

Is Posner still at the door, waiting with consent? The delay invites retribution upon us, for his explanation is less than satisfactory, and the consent involved is meagre compared with the rich tradition of political consent limiting kings and presidents. As a starting point, his drivers' insurance example is identified as a non-market transaction, since it offers only limited choices for risk prevention, and therefore lacks an essential market element for efficiency theory. It is still subject to wealth-maximizing, but we are asked first by Posner to consider a market-oriented choice embracing the following:

Assume a company closes its plant to move for better conditions from City A to City B. The company shareholders gain from the move. City A residents lose in property values. City B residents gain in property values. Three types of efficiency fare as follows:

1 Pareto-superiority does not work because there is a loser, the City A residents.
2 A special version of Pareto, known to economists as the Kaldor-Hicks efficiency criterion, is satisfied, because it contains a proviso that winners in such cases will, under government auspices, compensate losers on a Pareto basis. Total wealth increases and there are no losers.
3 Wealth-maximizing theory, Posner version, says put not your trust in government guarantees and declares the proviso a political matter, off-limits. Instead the preferred criterion is wealth-maximization, deriving consent from Pareto but forfeiting the 'no losers' restraint. Result: company shareholders and City B residents are winners; City A residents are losers; but society as a whole maximizes wealth.

12

Why should City A accept its losses and why should Posner find his version of wealth-maximizing ethically compelling? The answer begins with Posner acknowledging consent as basic to normal Pareto-superiority on a one-to-one bargaining basis (as it is for unimpeded bargaining generally), and as an ideal but illusory condition of larger transactions, such as product markets. In the larger transactions, Posner finds third-party effects (substitute commodities, imports) are so prevalent that consent of all involved would be impossible to negotiate. This impossible, illusory condition results in Pareto-superiority being of limited use for theory construction, including Pareto's original intent of solving the problem of utilitarianism as being unable to determine the interpersonal preferences of social goods. Even so, Posner finds in the concept of Pareto's 'consent' enough ethical substance to place it in the Kantian philosophic tradition, and from there in his own system of wealth-maximizing, validating his claim for an ethically compelling system.

Kantian moral philosophy places special emphasis on autonomy, treating people as self-directed individuals. Consent is an autonomous act, qualifying for a Kantian moral relationship. Did the losers in City A, example 3 above, consent to their losses? Yes, affirms Posner, but not expressly, only by implication. In economic analysis, one can consent to a loss by possession of prior (*ex ante*) knowledge of the risks one takes. A lottery ticket or an investment in the stock market involves similar 'consent' to losses, absent fraud. The same view of risk, of which we had a preview with Coase's hapless wheat farmers, is taken towards the residents of City A. They bought their land with the prior knowledge that the plant might be moved and this, in the world of efficient bargaining, must have been reflected in a discount in their purchase prices. These assertions can be disturbing, and call for more foundations, but Posner relies on additional legal precedents, particularly in common law, for his implied consent, leaving each of us to reflect on the ethical linkage.

Finally, consider the non-market system driver who is injured in an accident in which neither driver was at fault. Has the injured driver consented to not being compensated under the 'negligence' system (one that pays only for negligent driving claims), such as Posner advocates as being more efficient than a 'strict liability' system (one

13

that pays for all claims)? Posner asks us to stipulate, intuitively, that all drivers will gladly accept the new system on the grounds that it will cost less. Now comes a special version of consent. Consent is implied as a waiver of compensation where neither driver is at fault because any driver who wanted to be sure of compensation could buy first-person accident insurance, covering himself only, beforehand (*ex ante* again), to supplement his limited liability policy. Result: total cost of accident policies will increase, total cost of liability policies will decrease, but the sum total will be less than under the old system, reflecting another win for a wealth-maximizing society.[11]

Such selective analysis may appear dismissive, an attempt to portray economic analysis as an operating tool for an ideal republic of inspired bookkeepers. Cost versus benefits analysis, it may be assumed, is an efficiency criterion of general consensus, without need of further embellishment. It is mandatory for the environmental crisis, for world hunger, and no doubt for the future of capitalism itself. But can such a principle be transformed into a governing criterion for economic justice?

Posner's distinguished career as law professor, scholarly author, literary critic, and now federal Court of Appeals judge, places him beyond easy reach. Besides, he reminds us to take his ethical theory in the spirit intended, as a subject of speculation.[12] And whereas we have concentrated for our purposes on his brief excursion into economic justice theory, under the hazardous title of 'wealth-maximizing', the major thrust of his economic analysis is in relation to law. Judge Posner helped to establish this relationship, has written extensively on it, and has influenced a generation of lawyers and judges to consider such economic matters as costs, benefits, and efficiency in making judicial choices.

A 1989 court of appeals decision, *International Union* v. *Johnson Controls*, illustrates Posner and economic analysis of law in action. The case involves the employer's exclusion of women from jobs in which unborn children would be at risk from lead poisoning, ironically bringing charges of discrimination in hiring under the Civil Rights Act of 1964. The employer won the case. In his dissenting opinion, Posner argued that if employers could not prohibit women from certain dangerous jobs, potential liability could drive them out of business.

14

Rights would win a hollow victory, with firms like Johnson losing the market to imports from competitors with little concern for fetal safety or women's welfare. His morally-based, efficiency alternative: find a way to interpret anti-discrimination laws, which already have some exceptions, to include fetal protection. The Supreme Court reversed the Court of Appeals in 1991, disregarding Posner's alternative.[13]

A major premise of economic analysis of law is the important role such analysis played in the development of common law in the English court system. It is Posner's belief that the common law judges consistently rendered decisions that harmonized with efficient wealth-maximization, rather than redistribution, a distinctly different enterprise existing beyond their expected limits of judicial neutrality. The above-noted principle of consent was also firmly rooted in common law. It helped to determine the validity of contracts and thus restrained those judges from engaging in redistribution through reducing the obligations of those who might want to violate contracts for a better deal. Redistribution relates to a competing ethical principle, which we will meet inevitably in the course of this book.

A further consideration about the boundaries of capitalism is raised by Posner's cost-analysis theory. Where does market efficiency reach the point at which it should give way to moral considerations? What are the unrecorded health costs, for example, borne by the residents of Pittsburgh before the pollution of steel mills in that city was brought under control?

Notes

1 The availability of marketplace information becomes a matter of super-power failure, not just economic theory, for Senator Daniel P. Moynihan. 'In the end, the Soviet economy couldn't work because it was based on the rationing of information, and by definition that won't work.' (Interview with Alfred R. Hunt, Washington Bureau Chief, *Wall Street Journal*, 22 October 1990). Moynihan adds that US intelligence equally missed available information about Soviet economic power and political stability by creating its own system of secrecy.

2 Ronald H. Coase, 'The Problem of Social Cost', 3 *Journal of Law and*

Economics, 1 (1960). At age 81, Coase won the $1 million Nobel Prize in Economics for 1991. Professor emeritus at the University of Chicago's law school, he brought to economic theory concepts of property rights and 'transactions costs' that could lead to more efficient operation of the economy. The concepts gave an intellectual base to privatization of public enterprises.

3 Charles Fried, *Right and Wrong* (Cambridge, Mass.: Harvard University Press, 1978), 86–107. Fried criticizes the Coase theorem and economic analysis generally. The criteria of efficiency and indeterminate rights yield a vision of slave laborers bargaining for freedom and victims negotiating with rapists. Without moral foundations (bargainers and rights in economic analysis are morally neutral), the project fails. 'If intentionally harming an innocent person is wrong then that is why the act should be condemned and compensation exacted.'

4 *United States* v. *Carroll Towing Co.* 159 F. 2nd 169 (2nd Cir. 1947). Conway v. O'Brien, 111 F. 2nd 611 (2nd Cir. 1940).

5 For an excellent recent defense of reconstructed utilitarianism, giving all objectors their day in court, see Russell Hardin, *Morality within the Limits of Reason* (Chicago: University of Chicago Press, 1988).

6 Richard A. Posner, *The Economics of Justice* (Cambridge, Mass.: Harvard University Press, 1981, 2nd ed.), 98.

7 See Gary Wills, *Inventing America: Jefferson's Declaration of Independence* (Garden City, N.Y.: Doubleday, 1978), Chapters 10 and 8. See also Albert O. Hirschman, *Shifting Involvements: Private Interests and Public Action* (Princeton, N.J.: Princeton University Press, 1982), 122.

8 For a provocative analysis of power relationships in capitalism, see the recent work of Robert Heilbroner. In *The Nature and Logic of Capitalism* (New York: W.W. Norton & Co., 1985), chapters 2, 3, the continuous urge to amass wealth is seen as initiating a concurrent drive for power, partly for social control over labor, partly for distinction and prestige. In *Behind the Veil of Economics* (New York: W.W. Norton & Co., 1988), 30–3, Heilbroner pursues the idea by enlisting the subconscious, suggesting that the conventional idea of a free market responding to rational self-interest might instead be a market tamed by 'habitual subordination' to accept unrecognized domination. Charles E. Lindblom's classic *Politics and Markets* (New York: Basic Books, 1977), defines western capitalist countries as 'polyarchies' rather than 'democracies', with social mechanisms

(large corporations and property interests) exercising undue power over the economic market system, inhibiting necessary structural reforms.

9 Alasdair MacIntyre, *After Virtue* (Notre Dame: University of Notre Dame Press, 1984, 2nd ed.), 50. MacIntyre proposes that classic moral philosophers, Aristotle in particular, correctly viewed man's perspective of the world as purposeful (teleological) and community-bound, providing a context for self-improvement as well as the combining of factual analysis with moral evaluation. Modern concepts of individual moral autonomy (Kierkegaard, Kant, Hume), discarding teleology, divine authority and hierarchy, cast consensual ethics adrift, leaving its agents unable to justify or debate widely varying principles for action. The charge is repeated in his *Whose Justice? Which Rationality?* (Notre Dame: University of Notre Dame Press, 1988), 6–9.

10 For a strong presentation by a sociologist on behalf of a normative concept of society, see Derek L. Phillips, *Towards a Just Social Order* (Princeton: Princeton University Press, 1986).

11 Posner, *Economics of Justice*, 96.

12 Ibid., vi.

13 *International Union* v. *Johnson Controls*, 89 F. 7th 1215 (7th Cir.) 1989. On 21 March 1991, the US Supreme Court reversed the Appeals Court decision on a 6–3 vote. Justice Harry A. Blackmun, writing for the majority, excluded fetal protection on the grounds of sex bias prohibited by federal civil rights law. Scant attention was paid to the efficiency problems of business as broadly considered in Judge Posner's Appeals Court dissenting opinion. Minority Justices Rehnquist, White and Kennedy said fetal protection policies should be judged case-by-case, permitting exclusion when 'reasonably necessary' to protect employers from lawsuits.

2 The virtues: an analogue of personal behavior

1 Moral Theory Construction

Why should we approach our subject indirectly in terms of analogues? Are we ready to come to grips with the main issue, the moral limitations of capitalism? Yes, but first we must explore morality, the more elusive of the two concepts. We understand the reality of capitalism. It controls our getting and spending. Moreover, it is a peculiarly modern institution, firmly embedded in modern traditions and consciousness, quick to shed its infirmities and obsolete techniques. Morality is a different story. It is a cumulative behavioral inheritance of diverse standards, embedded in past cultures and traditions, from Homer's age of warrior ethics to our own of moral pluralism.

The paradox of past moralities invading the present resonates in our common speech and public discourse. From the medieval age of belief we still bid 'goodbye' ('God be with ye') and use currency entrusted to God. From the eighteenth-century Enlightenment period we recall natural law, the source of moral law for the Stoics, when we read the Preamble to the Declaration. The specifications of a just war, formulated by St. Augustine and St. Thomas Aquinas in the Catholic tradition, were publicly compelling when revived in the moral debate over the Persian Gulf War, at least on the item of proportionality, or limits on the means used to achieve goals.[1] It should be a commonplace that our view of the world, and hence our related moral norms and standards, are primarily shaped by the particular cultures we live in and which we have inherited, as well as by the meanings we attach to key words in our changing language, such as the virtue words we will consider herein.

Some additional conclusions can be drawn at this point relating to the observations on moral theory construction introduced in Chapter 1. Even in the face of such powerful cultural determination of values, which offer a strong case for moral relativism, moral theorists on balance are likely to be certainty-seekers. After all, their constituency has an insatiable demand, based on need as individuals and parents, for moral guidance, moral comfort and moral limits, not moral dilemmas. It is a rare life that does not write its own moral narrative if one survives long enough in normal circumstances, let alone the precarious life-settings of the great majority. This narrative would include not only how one experiences the anticipated ravages of nature, but also first, what the Romans called *fortuna*, the deadweight of fate or luck, and second, the fragility of goodness, which conversely acknowledges the durability of evil.[2] It would not be a morality tale, of the type told by Chaucer or Dante for exemplary purposes, but a roll call of moral claims, or cries, inherent in the human condition. Calling to mind this lifetime demand, and its sober components, leads to the prospect that the average person would see little value in half-measures or uncertainty when offered moral prescriptions.

Moral theorists disdain the standards of average persons, but it is clear they have responded to the need for certainty in two directions. The theorist may reach for certainty by extending his grasp all the way to absolute, unconditional injunctions in the form of principles, maxims and rules of a timeless and universal nature. Or he may take a less determinate direction towards relative, less rigid standards of morality. The common denominator in either case would be claims of authority, or certainty, based on the moral theory's objective being justified because it was rationally reached, regardless of agreement on the validity of the objective itself. For example, Kant's absolutist, obligatory objective of exemplary morality attained through the exercise of 'autonomous will', and Aristotle's less rigorous objective of a state of 'well-being', may equally claim the certainty that rests on the rational justification attached to the process used to reach these objectives. This does not mean the rational use of inductive or deductive logic is necessarily involved.[3] But it involves at a minimum the use of 'rational reflection', the process of deliberately stepping back from a subject, subjecting it to intellectual scrutiny, and claiming thereby sufficient objectivity or certainty, in terms of timelessness and generality, or possibly universality. Thus the process leading to the moral theory's fundamental objective, and generally the principles of its operations as well, stand up to reason, the supreme arbiter of philosophy.

The employment of 'right, good reason' as the Greeks fondly called this intellectual weapon against the prevailing superstitions, helps to explain why philosophy, originally a pagan enterprise, feels it must exclude religion from moral theory. It is ironical that a discipline concerned with ethics from Socrates onward should, largely because of philosophy's rationalist birthright, later reinforced by the harsh secular bias of the Enlightenment period, draw a veil over religion, surely our most pervasive and durable institutional moral influence, however flawed its history. We will weigh in a strong religious intermediary for morality in economic institutions in Chapter 8.

The irony is increased by the current decline in reason's fortunes, at least in moral theory, as stated in Chapter 1. Moral theories appear to go in and out of fashion with the same inconstancy as theories of medicine and economics. Still the fall from grace of reason, considering how much is invested in concepts such as rational justification, represents a major shift in moral theory. Philosophy itself remains reason-centered, with logic, dialectic and non-contradictory, coherent discourse its favorite fare. Its Greek name, 'love of wisdom', clearly affirms its foundation in rational inquiry.

Considerations of ethics and morality, however, relate to the inexact, often irrational, field of human behavior. As such these subsections of philosophy have always been recognized as dealing with a conflict of emotions and rational restraints, of 'the passions versus the interests', and similar 'good and bad' dichotomies.[4] Most moral theory concepts of modern times, from the sixteenth century onward, result in reason's ultimate triumph in such struggles; otherwise no progress, no bonds of community, and no order for society are considered possible. There have been important skeptics on the matter, such as David Hume, who contended that 'reason is and always must be the slave of the passions.' His intentions, however, were not to endorse the supremacy of the passions, but to advocate their diversion into useful channels, including the interests of emerging capitalism, rather than the passions of political and religious wars.[5] Relying on the redundancy that a society is no better than its individuals, we can concentrate for the moment on the 'ethics philosophers', for whom personal conduct is paramount, and place on hold our ultimate concern, the 'justice philosophers', introduced in Chapter 1, who are primarily concerned with social justice and thus with capitalism. Interestingly Aristotle, the founding father of ethics morality, and the connoisseur of the moral virtues, would take exception to this division of labor among theorists. Among his remarkable talents, he was our first behavioral scientist, possessing a sociologist's sharp eye for individual differences and motivations. But he also viewed man as a 'political animal' and felt a solid, primary identity with his beloved *polis*, the Athenian city-state of approximately 250,000 population, including a reported 80,000 slaves and 30,000 resident foreigners who carried on its daily work.[6] In brief he expected the virtuous citizens of his aristocratic, privileged world to share his statist loyalties and obligations, leading to a particular concept of the virtues, the unitary 'all or none' requirement, which on its face is unacceptable for modern subscribers, who look askance at paragons of virtue. Those who long for a return to so-called Aristotelian values should recall the ambience in which his civic virtue flourished, and keep in mind that other similarly intense fusions of public and private virtue have inevitably failed.

* * *

Books about 'limits' flourish, both in economics and moral theory. The underlying reason in economics could well be the universal change in consciousness arising from the recognition of environmental limitations, that planet Earth is threatened. In Chapter 1, we proposed the need for a moral evaluation, above and beyond the favorable consequences of the market system, for the distribution of economic resources in a capitalist system. Economists traditionally define such a distribution as the allocation of 'scarce' or finite resources, but it is only with the recent emphasis on limits ('the limits to growth', the 'zero-sum society', etc.) that relative scarcity is viewed as more than a hypothetical condition affecting market and price functions. Analogously, political theorists are concerned with the limits of central government and debt, sociologists with the limits of welfarism and punishment, and scientists with the limits of weapons and medical experimentation.

2 Aristotle's Rise and Reason's Decline

Turning to moral theory, Bernard Williams, author of *Ethics and the Limits of Philosophy* (1985), has considered the issues of Aristotle's rise and reason's decline. Williams is one of the most admired of contemporary ethics philosophers, teaching with distinction in both England and America. For Williams, the limits of philosophy mean basically the limits of reason. A thorough man of reason himself, Williams confines his criticism to the inadequacy of reason as the grounding, or justifying, force of ethical theories. Selecting from his complex analysis may do him injustice, but he sees, for example, a great divide between the reason of the ancient and modern worlds. The world of Aristotle may have had a minor obsession about reducing exposure to *fortuna*, or luck, but it did not, like the modern world from Kant onward, obsessively impose rationality on moral theory in a reductive, all-or-nothing manner. If we are persuaded by this point of view, we tend to look favorably on Aristotle's moderately relativist moral theory, which requires neither moral purity nor unconditional demands for entry into ethical life.[7]

Williams further holds 'the failure of the Enlightenment' to be an impediment for modern moral theory. He does not expand on this assertion but the inference is that Enlightenment reason is enshrined and carried to excess in modern thought.[8] For perspective, Alasdair MacIntyre, Williams' eminent colleague and a leading authority in contemporary moral virtue studies, rejects Enlightenment philosophy (such notions as liberalism, individualism, rationalism and progress) out of hand. MacIntyre, however, is an intense anti-individualist, has a compelling interest in order and traditions, and appears to prefer the pre-modern world, whereas Williams is very much a pro-individualist and firmly planted in the present.

Both men, however, share a special view of modern rationality as 'bureaucratic', with disabling effects on moral action the predictable result. This concept views reason as being allied primarily with 'administrative' (Williams' term) or officially-based choices for action, excluding ethically-based choices accordingly. This results in most of the important choices being made or influenced by rational but ethically-warped public figures.[9] An archetype of the morally-blinkered, rational bureaucrat would surely be Adolf Eichmann, the Nazi functionary, as described by Hannah Arendt in *Eichmann in Jerusalem: A Report on the Banality of Evil* (1983). Franz Kafka's *The Trial* and Gian Carlo Menotti's *The Consul* also make the point about bureaucracy, reminding us that morality may best be learned outside the classroom.

The view of modern rationality as bureaucratically antipathetic to the ethical life resembles Max Weber's concept of the modern political state as essentially a web of shallow bureaucratic relationships arising from the functional requirements of widespread organization. Utilitarianism, directing its rational energies towards the best social consequences and thereby, according to its critics, placing individual moral considerations at risk, is a moral theory that, considering these constraints, has successfully accommodated itself to such a corporate world. ('Morality,' Bentham allegedly said, 'is nonsense on stilts.')

Though skeptical, Williams is steadfast in his search for an ethical life suitable for the conditions of modern knowledge and consciousness. Long an opponent of utilitarianism, he finds reason in the Kantian alternative located in the area of abstraction, no better off than utilitarianism's placement in the bureaucratic structure. Kant's notion of a 'republic of reason', in which we individually make moral choices, but only through maxims or rules to which we believe all men would universally subscribe, is too abstract for Williams, too far removed from social and historical reality, disconnected from a concrete sense of an individual's daily, earthbound life. Utilitarian reason is thus too involved in worldly affairs, and Kantian reason is too far removed from them, for Williams' approval.

What then is suitable for modern man's moral guidance, given such limitations? What is the answer, Williams asks, to Socrates' question, 'How should one live?' Briefly, Williams' account of reason's decline and Aristotle's revival appear to converge in his answer. Williams is hopeful on two prospects. First, he hopes for the primacy of the individual, and second, he hopes that these individuals will acquire dispositions to character that will lead them to an ethical life.

Williams' 'dispositions to character' have their origin in the function assigned by Aristotle to the virtues. For Aristotle the shaping of character underlies the elaborate listing of virtues in the *Nichomachean Ethics*, named after his editor-son, Nichomachus. Recall that Aristotle had discerned a goal-oriented, biological urge among humans to achieve a state of happiness, or 'well-being', through a process of self-perfection, or pursuit of excellence. Now he calls upon the resources of philosophy, subsection ethics, to provide a technique for accomplishing this purposeful goal, the cultivation of the virtues. Additionally, 'right, good reason' could further guide the virtue-disposed person to make ethically-based choices in actual practice, a fusion of reason and ethics called 'practical reason' by moral theorists thereafter.

Some observations should be made about Aristotle before we visit virtue in other time-frames and cultures. Aristotle in translation is presented in the complex, elliptical style of his unedited lecture notes. There is no need to examine the *Nichomachean Ethics* at this point other than note its four 'cardinal', or 'hinge', virtues (so-called because of their importance): justice, prudence, courage, and temperance. Socrates and Plato preceded Aristotle with special roles for the virtues but Aristotle substantively expanded the definitions and the analytical commentary. Additionally, each virtue is placed under a fundamental human 'sphere of action'. Courage, for example, is profoundly located within the sphere of 'fear of death'. Above all it is apparent that the virtues are not to be treated as instrumental or self-serving. That technique is relegated to the sophists, a rival group of means-oriented philosophers looked down upon by Aristotle and his circle (but triumphant once again among 'how-to' authors). The virtues instead are to be used to internalize or socialize patterns of action and temperament in an ethical direction, without thought of gain or reward.

Aristotle's moral theory is thus presented in the sense of its rational objective, a state of happiness or 'well-being', in its justification, nature's purpose for man to achieve a kind of self-perfection; and in its basic operative principle, the virtues as a technique for generating 'dispositions to character'. Add to this the Aristotelian injunction that one must maintain a long-range 'way of life' in this mode (less austere than religious prescriptions of this type but still involving total commitment) as a further operative principle, and the theory is reasonably coherent. It is also reasonably persuasive in ability to enlist consensus, another test imposed by theorists.

Is this theory, however reductively presented, adequate to justify claims of superiority, of approbation by authorities as distinguished as Williams, MacIntyre, Stuart Hampshire, Martha Nussbaum and Phillipa Foot? The answer depends on recognition that all such venerable theories become anachronistic, with the central thrust of their arguments, and the original brilliance and daring of their expositions, becoming the vital inheritance for later enthusiasts. This may be particularly the case when the alternative market includes not only the faulty utilitarian and Kantian models we have discussed, but the feckless existentialist model barely mentioned by the Aristotelian revivalists, who require at the very least adherence to moral principles and values.

Specifically, with Williams as a friend, Aristotle has little need for opponents. Before embracing Aristotle as philosopher of last resort, Williams is generous with criticism. He disparages Aristotle's 'unity of the virtues' requirement along the lines we have mentioned, with an additional warning against the need for artists and writers to conform with public virtue. He dismisses Aristotle's fundamental concept of a natural, teleological instinct for self-perfection leading to 'happiness' or 'well-being' as dubious meta-biology, although the down-to-earth goal of 'well-being' or 'flourishing', as the neo-Aristotelians choose to call it, still suffices as the objective for the ethical life. Williams reluctantly pardons Aristotle's regrettable blind-side on slavery, natural attributes and gender as a time-warp at best. He then demolishes a good deal of the structure of the virtues themselves. After all, what kind of paradigm is a 'great-souled man', schooled in Magnificence as the 'Mean' between the extremes of Vulgarity on the one hand and Pettiness on the other? Williams does not use this example, but as far as the time-honored doctrine of the

Golden Mean is concerned, incorporated at length by Aristotle in his table of virtues (and functioning as contraband against creative action ever since), he observes, 'the Mean is better forgotten.'[10]

What then, is the positive side of Aristotelian moral theory, justifying its resurgence? It is the central thrust of a value-concerned theory, grounded on human nature and experience, and related to individual flourishing rather than rewards, results, or transcendent moral absolutes. Moreover the theory offers ample opportunity for revision and improvement. For those who give priority to individual flourishing and character formation, such as Williams and Nussbaum, or advocate a constructive conflict between rationalism and imaginative emotions, such as Stuart Hampshire, Aristotle represents not only the best of the classics but a starting point on which to build, if one rejects eighteenth and twentieth-century alternatives.[11]

In the socioeconomic field, there has also been an Aristotelian boomlet. Here the linkage is more direct, for Aristotle, always at one with his beloved *polis*, is viewed as the great communitarian. In this sense, Adam Smith's concept of an economic man, born to barter, get and spend, in accord with his natural self-interest, would have troubled Aristotle, who not only disdained trade but viewed all such activities as completely subordinated to the interests of the *polis*, if not already to the paternally-ruled household. The 'great transformation', Karl Polanyi's term in his book of that name (1944), which severed this quasi-statist connection as nascent capitalism appeared, is a regrettable bifurcation in the eyes of prominent observers from the center left, such as George C. Lodge of Harvard Business School, and center right, such as Robert Nisbet of Columbia University. Both invoke Aristotle in their pleas for a return to a more communitarian and integrated society, one in which a crisis-ridden democracy presumably might again flourish.[12] Note that Williams, a moral philosopher, finds support for individualism in Aristotle's concern for man's fulfilment as a particular being. Lodge, a socioeconomist, finds support against individualism, in this case John Locke's individualism, which Lodge feels has sustained laissez-faire ideology, in Aristotle's priority for bonding with his fellow citizens. Such equivalence illustrates Aristotle's pragmatic approach to issues, as well as the fact that we tend to find in the ancient philosophers what we want to find.

26

The view from Aristotle's room is reinforced by the sensitive sociological analysis compiled by Robert N. Bellah and his co-authors in their *Habits of the Heart: Individualism and Commitment in American Life* (1985). Individualism for these researchers, who based their work on in-depth conversations with representative Americans in representative communities, no longer sustains commitment. Instead it appears, in its 'modern' form, at least, to be isolating Americans from each other, perhaps threatening the survival of freedom itself.[13]

The authors readily acknowledge their subjects are all white and middle-class, arguing the importance of this category in American culture. They remind us that from Aristotle onward, republican theorists have stressed the importance of the middle classes for the success of free institutions. (There is a grain of truth in this defense. Who would deny that John Updike's Rabbit Angstrom is the present-day essential American?)

Aristotle is further called on by Bellah for his analysis of friendship as the basis for community cohesion.[14] The *Nichomachean Ethics* do indeed define and measure friendship.[15] It has three aspects: friends must enjoy each others' company; they must be useful, including helping each other become better persons; and they must share a commitment to the common good. The second and third aspects, the moral components, are essential towards making the good society. There is circumspect information about male friendship in that distant culture that scholars have recently made available, but the conventional wisdom finds classical roots, such as the Aristotelian virtue of friendship, magnified by Christian theology, behind the roof-raising and volunteer militias of an earlier, warmer America.

It was this America that the astute French social philosopher Alexis de Tocqueville visited in the 1830s and analyzed so well in his *Democracy in America* (1835–1840). The Americans, he wrote, had two particular characteristics, somewhat in tension. The relation to the community, to interaction with others, was sustained by family life, religion, voluntary associations, and democratic politics, all healthy for the maintenance of freedom and its institutions. The other side of the American was his 'individualism'. Tocqueville was one of the first to use the word, which he associated with equality and thought might eventually isolate Americans from each other and undermine their community of freedom.[16] These disparate elements of the American ethos he termed 'habits of the heart', a variation of Aristotle's dispositions to character.

Notes

1 History will resolve these arguments, but it appears that President Bush was unable to rally sufficient support for a basically economic justification for the Persian Gulf War, oil resources, however effectively presented. The critical balance of public affirmation was in response to his moral reasons, to go to war for principles of freedom, self-determination, and a new world-order. None of these worthy items are in the seven specifications handed down for a 'just war', an illustration of how each period updates its moral principles.

2 For the narrative as guide to morality, see (other than the great writers themselves), MacIntyre, *After Virtue*, 142–45, 181–87, 239–43; Martha Nussbaum, *Love's Knowledge: Essays on Philosophy and Literature* (New York: Oxford University Press, 1990). Nussbaum asserts that since our capacity for ethical understanding involves emotional as well as intellectual capacity, we can well expand emotional capacity beyond the people and situations of daily experience by drawing on our heritage of significant literature. The novel especially reveals heightened human complexities, enlarging ethical insight into private and public life.

3 An authority for deductive logic as bearing on the decision process can be found in Aristotle's 'practical syllogism'. Alasdair MacIntyre analyzes this process as a parallel to Aristotle's theoretical syllogism. If one sees *a*, is a good action and *b*, circumstances are propitious for same, then *c*, the practical syllogism completes itself by demanding immediate action. MacIntyre approves of such capacity for action, as against modern tendencies to mull things over (e.g. Rawls's 'reflective equilibrium'), and attributes it to traditional, assigned roles in the pre-modern period, in which morally-oriented people react directly, like good chess or hockey players do today. Many 'Aristotelians' differ with MacIntyre. MacIntyre, *Whose Justice? Which Rationality?* 138–43.

4 Albert O. Hirschman, *The Passions and The Interests: Political Arguments for Capitalism before Its Triumph* (Princeton: Princeton University Press, 1977); Fried, *Right and Wrong*.

28

5 Hirschman, *The Passions and The Interests*, 24–6.

6 M.I. Finley, *The Ancient Greeks* (New York: Penguin Books, 1977), 72; *Ancient Slavery & Modern Ideology* (New York: The Viking Press, 1980), 80; Orlando Patterson, *Slavery and Social Death* (Cambridge, Mass.: Harvard University Press, 1982), 354.

7 Martha Nussbaum reminds us that Aristotle's relativist 'virtue ethics' do not prevent him from being strongly concerned with the idea that certain core virtues, like justice, have a normative function. See Martha Nussbaum, 'Non-Relativist Virtues: An Aristotelian Approach', in Peter A. French, *et al.*, eds., *Midwest Studies in Philosophy*, vol. XIII (Notre Dame: University of Notre Dame Press, 1988), 32–53. Nussbaum has cautioned me to note that Aristotelian ethical philosophers may be seen as generally dividing along positions with deep differences. Those emphasizing Aristotelian bonding and collective identification with public norms, such as MacIntyre and Bellah, embrace essentially conservative, communitarian principles; on the other hand, Nussbaum and Amartya Sen (for additional example), derive from Aristotle's concern for individual ethical flourishing a demand for less inequality and more social justice to achieve such flourishing in contemporary life. (See 70 *Texas Law Review* 971 [March 1992], in which both Judge Posner and Nussbaum define such issues.)

8 Bernard Williams, *Ethics and the Limits of Philosophy* (Cambridge, Mass.: Harvard University Press, 1985), 198.

9 *Ibid.*, 197; MacIntyre, *After Virtue*, claims modern moral authority has been abandoned to elite characters such as the 'aesthete', (24–5), the 'therapist', (73–4), and the 'bureaucratic expert', (75–6); also see chap. 1, fn 8, *supra*.

10 *Ibid.*, 36.

11 See Stuart Hampshire, *Morality and Conflict*, (Cambridge, Mass.: Harvard University Press, 1983), in which a two-tiered ethics system is proposed, based on Aristotelian rationalism in useful conflict with emotional and artistic feelings. (It is only a matter of time before moral theorists advocating conflict theory might hold anatomical research on their side. These researchers, based on conclusive animal studies, propose that the ties in the human brain between the rational cognitive, via the cortex, and the emotional, via the amygdala, together always shape what we perceive as well as what we remember. See Mortimer Mishkin, National Institute of Mental Health, *Los Angeles Times*, 24 June 1991, B3.)

12 George C. Lodge, *The New American Ideology* (New York: Alfred A. Knopf, 1976), 46–51; Robert Nisbet, *The Social Philosophers* (New York: Thomas Y. Crowell, 1973), 3, 390–96.

13 Robert N. Bellah, *Habits of the Heart* (Berkeley, Calif.: University of California Press, 1985), viii.

14 *Ibid.*, 116.

15 Aristotle, *Nichomachean Ethics*, Books 8,9.

16 Alexis de Tocqueville, *Democracy in America* (New York: Schocken Books, 1961, originally published 1835–40), vol. 2, 124–25.

3 The virtues in historical context

This chapter will consider the virtues concept in three selected historical periods. The unifying theory is the consistent transformation of the concept by the host cultures. Additionally the selected periods are highly visible in our historical imaginations, so the enjoyment of recognition is possible, facilitating concentration on the arcane subject matter.

1 The Virtues in Homeric Society

As noted, any overview of the virtues in moral theory starts with Aristotle as the central authority. Aristotle's view of the ancient world was the world of Homer's *Iliad*, and the differences between the virtues concepts of Homer and Aristotle reflect Aristotle's ability to transcend and improvise within the Homeric tradition. It was a tradition still vibrant in his Hellenic world, preceding the empires of Alexander and Rome.

The *Iliad* as heroic epic can be read for its narrative and poetry alone. We can follow Keats, who, 'on first looking into Chapman's Homer', lost himself in the great adventures of the 'pure serene', not in sociology. Still, most authorities believe the *Iliad* fairly describes what is called Homeric society, dating about 1200 BC (the siege of Troy), a period far earlier than Homer's own lifetime, which is assumed to be just prior to 700 BC. Role and status are predetermined in Homeric society, much as they are in the medieval period of knights and vassals, millennia later. Values are what one would expect in a static culture, where the key social structures are kinship and the household, and the basic ethos the warrior temperament. The leading virtues accordingly include concepts such as honor, duty, obligation, and friendship. It is not a reflective or reasoning society. Actions are the measure of a man, not his words, nor his dispositions. The word for 'virtue', *arete*, is used in the Homeric poems to connote only 'excellence'. It does not have the ethical context it would acquire in Athenian Greece.

Prudence, later to be esteemed as the queen of virtues, is slighted in favor of cunning, entitled to special glory, (*kudos*), when warriors hide in the gift of a wooden horse. Friendship has special value in a society of feuds and retaliation. Friends take vows of brotherhood and can reach the legendary relationship of Achilles and Patroclus.

Justice beyond a primitive stage (those who kill get killed) is absent, although this virtue is not unknown in the Mediterranean world of Homer's reported lifetime. The Hebrew prophets were already demanding just personal lives and social justice. Their Decalogue, laws of behavior, and Messianic prophecy would become a groundswell of creativity sufficient to conquer Rome itself. The point is not to compare Homer with prophets unknown to him, nor to suggest that he should have rewritten the great narrative handed down to him. But one can measure Homer against the theory that writers are inescapably bound to their manuscripts subjectively and that all great works of literature invariably have some moral content, reflecting the writer's point of view.

Although the embryonic virtue of justice may be unavailable for reconciling the myriad of contentious claims in the *Iliad*, Homer can be shown as subjectively and philosophically involved in other matters. For example, consider an additional leading virtue in Homeric society, courage. As in other heroic societies, courage is actually the supreme virtue, which may explain its survival, alone from the Homeric period, as a cardinal virtue throughout the centuries.[1] Courage, as we have noted in Aristotle's cataloging, finds it sharpest need in the face of death. Death is omnipresent in the *Iliad*, and it is reasonable to believe that the concept of death as the great leveller, wherein roles are eliminated, is the poet's insight, not that of his characters. More subtly, Homer puts into question the matter of winning and losing. Is there any victory which is not also a loss, he asks, in the sense that one's own time for defeat or death is ineluctable?

Simone Weil (1909–1943), the French philosopher and Catholic mystic, analyzes the *Iliad* as essentially a poem of force but also of deep moral significance in a posthumous work translated by Mary McCarthy.[2] In the *Iliad*'s world of unrelenting, pitiless force, she sees Homer's even-handed treatment of victors and victims, of war and peace, as a triumph of perception, of seeing things as they really are. This clarity of vision she regards as the greatest antidote to self-deception, which she believes lies at the heart of failed moral conduct.

This element of perception in Greek thought, perfected by the tragic playwrights, led the Greeks to a sense of retribution (*nemesis*), operating with geometric rigor, measure for measure, as a penalty for the excessive use of force. It is a conception of limits, or equilibrium, which is no longer influential in the conduct of western life, she claims, suffused as that life is with material objectives. 'We are only geometricians of matter; the Greeks were, first of all, geometricians in their apprenticeship to virtue.'[3]

2 St. Thomas Aquinas and the Expansion of the Virtues

One of the greatest figures in intellectual history is St. Thomas Aquinas (1225–1274). The 'angelic doctor', whose synthesis for harmonizing Greek rationalism with Christian divine belief became official church doctrine, paid special attention to the virtues in his *Summa theologica* (1267–1273).

In his novel *The Name of the Rose*, Umberto Eco presupposes the omnipresence of Aristotle in the medieval consciousness for his story of murder in the early fourteenth-century monasteries. It centers on the existence of a secret, newly-discovered manuscript of Aristotle, endorsing the virtues of humor and laughter. The revolutionary manuscript not only challenges the institutional asceticism but Augustinian doctrinal gloom as well. It could be used as evidence against the Aristotelians believed to be subverting church theology, both within and outside its walls.

It is tempting to think of Thomas, his intellect fired by the priority of reason among classic philosophers, as a budding Aristotelian when he entered his first of a series of church-dominated universities, the University of Paris, in 1245, after being forcibly detained at home for a year by an uncooperative father. The universities of Europe had experienced a period of growth, creativity, and new levels of freedom in the twelfth century. They were attended by international students communicating in a common, scholarly language, the Latin of Virgil, Cicero and the church fathers. Theology, Aquinas's choice, was only one of the areas of concentration. Law was the most popular, then as now the avenue to employment in the institutions surrounding church and state.

The great rediscovery of Aristotle's major body of long-forgotten works, including the *Nichomachean Ethics*, had only recently been completed, largely from translations from the Arabic copies that had been maintained in the Islamic intellectual world. By Thomas's time, new translations directly from the Greek were available. Aristotelian ideas were very much in play, the subjects of intense debate.

In fact Thomas's role was to be not only harmonizer between classical reason and Augustinian faith, but also between contending schools of Aristotelian adherents. On the extreme or radical side of the latter, as far as church authority was concerned, was the Islamic tradition itself, personified by its two greatest translators, Avicenna, a Persian (Ibn Sina) of the early eleventh century, and Averroës, a Spaniard (Ibn Rushd) of the late twelfth century, almost contemporary with Thomas. In brief terms, Avicenna's cosmology was the natural, mechanistic world of Aristotle, with its concept of an infinitely regressive original causation of the cosmos, contradicting creation theory. In this universe, God is a generating force, or Intelligence, in the Platonic sense. He is not the intervening, interfering Judeo-Christian God, omniscient and receptive to individual prayers. If that were not sufficiently heretical, for an authoritarian, revealed system, consider the implications of Averroism. Averroës, the greatest of the Muslim philosophers, was the preeminent Aristotelian scholar of his time, not only in the Arabic world, but in a large part of the Latin Christian world as well. Aquinas refers to him simply as the Commentator in his own writings. On the basic question of how one can reconcile one's stake in science with the requirements of faith posed by the Koran, Averroës has a startling answer for both Muslims and Christians. If science demonstrates the eternity of the world and thereby denies the creation doctrine, then the claims of science and faith are irreconcilable. The solution to the contradiction is to accept the existence of a 'double-truth', one for science and one for faith. For extra measure, Averroës denies personal immortality and upholds the doctrine of the universal soul, another Aristotelian concept guaranteed to offend.

The Averroist radicalism which Thomas was to accommodate so brilliantly in his *Summa* and other writings had already been banished in the Islamic world. Ironically Averroës had infuriated Muslim orthodoxy sufficiently to secure his own condemnation from the new puritanical political powers in North Africa, successors to the Golden Age of Muslim Spain. In a sense, Aquinas, incorporating what he could of the great Arabic scholar's interpretation in his own system, preserved an essential contribution to western philosophy.

A similar rejection was experienced by some of the best minds of Jewish medieval thought. Again the problem was the gap between reason and faith. Spanish Jews rose to high positions in government and commerce, and prospered in the learned professions, particularly in medicine, in tenth and eleventh-century Muslim Spain, while their European brethren were being persecuted and ghettoized. Maimonides (1135–1204), was the epitome of the unchallenged Talmudic scholar and physician to viziers in this cultivated world. Devoted to Aristotle and the inescapable truths of science, he set out to guide the perplexed, as he entitled one of his works, on how to bridge the gap between Talmudic knowledge and Aristotelian reason. As Thomas was to do after him, he rejected Averroës's double-truth doctrine; only a single God-given truth was available. Still the remaining Aristotelian concepts of a partially mechanistic cosmos and a general rather than individual condition of immortality in his analyses were sufficient to induce the legalistic and fundamentalist rabbinate of his own community to denounce this estimable man as a heretic, and to ban his philosophical works.

Only by such comparisons does Thomas's experience appear favorable. The 'angelic doctor', so-called because of his calm and impartial demeanor (reinforced by his robust girth), was not immediately acclaimed by his peers and church. His position was attacked by the bishop of Paris and by the leading contemporary philosophers of the Dominicans, his own order, at Oxford. Additionally, St. Bonaventura, head of the rival Franciscan order, which dominated theology at Oxford, had published a major treatise advancing the Platonic-Augustinian position against the new Aristotelianism. His opponents claimed the complex, ordered, systematic and logically argued philosophy of theology summarized on behalf of the church by Thomas had rejected Augustine for Aristotle. It had downgraded the primacy of the will for that of the intellect. After due deliberation, Thomas was canonized in 1323, proclaimed Doctor of the Church in 1567 and his system finally declared the official Catholic philosophy (though not exclusively) in 1879.

* * *

The virtues appear continually throughout the *Summa*, a project intended to cover all aspects of one's life, not just the spiritual. Scholars with an interest in statistics count 170 separate 'questions', (each a minor essay), covering over a million words on the subject.[4] We will discuss briefly the methodology and the significance of the content.

Thomas's method is that of the scholastic teacher. In each instance a basic question is asked, which is promptly answered in the negative, supported by cogent, enumerated arguments attributed to eminent authorities, usually the apostles, church fathers, the Philosopher (Aristotle), and the Commentator. Aquinas then changes roles and becomes advocate for the affirmative side, the true answer, which he establishes by marshalling even more convincing positions and rebuttals, typically from the same authorities, fortified by his own subtle dialectic. The methodology becomes a command performance of classical, biblical and theological expertise. The scrupulous attention paid to the defeated position is disarming. But the constant appeals to divine authority for otherwise untenable assertions produce simulacra of rigged courtroom proceedings for the modern mind.

Like Aristotle, Aquinas is a relentless cataloger. He starts simply enough, with the four cardinal, or natural, virtues, and the three theological virtues, faith, hope and charity (love), at the top of his ladder. The natural virtues can be acquired, but the theological virtues can only be infused, or poured in, by God's grace. Each of the seven virtues contains multiple categories and subcategories of additional virtues, in descending order of relationship to the primary virtue. As with dictionary definitions, those toward the bottom of the ladder become increasingly marginal. For example, the virtue of *gnome*, or knowing when to make an exception to a rule, traces upward to the cardinal virtue of practical wisdom, or prudence. Wearing the cap of philosopher, Aquinas appears to take delight in examining the nuances of the classical inheritance.

The highly organized and systematic list enables him to analyze resemblances and differences among the virtues and above all to illustrate how the natural virtues support and reinforce the theological virtues. Thus the virtue of friendship, which we have seen was highly valued, though for varying reasons, in Homeric Greece, in the *Nichomachean Ethics*, and in Tocqueville's America, receives a special role from Aquinas. The virtue of charity is described by Aquinas in terms of Aristotle's concept of ideal friendship, a process wherein the Philosopher and his virtue are mediated into the Christian virtue analogically. Charity is characterized by a sharing of 'desires' with God, a wish to share the companionship, joy, and other attributes of a true Aristotelian friendship. There are those who will find the analogy contrived, a fault not unusual to lay at Thomas's door.

Aquinas as cataloger would hold little interest. Largely because of such inventorying, Renaissance humanists dismissed the scholastics as pedants concerned with how many angels might stand on the head of a pin. Defenders remind us that the humanists lacked comprehension of the medieval world-view, and that decisions affecting the patiently crafted balance between Platonic philosophy and Christian theology were critical in a time of religious and intellectual intensity. Basic to Plato's legacy was a belief in the reality of ideas, or universals, that ideas or concepts have an independent reality of their own, existing outside the human being and his mental apparatus. That Plato, a paradigm of reason, could conceive of the independent reality of such a concept as God himself was a comforting prospect to Christian theologians. They found reason supporting what they accepted through faith and revelation.

Simplified though this 'realist' version may be, there is little doubt the arguments to the contrary by the 'nominalists', that such ideas were without independent reality, and represented only names and terms facilitating discussion, were unsettling. Peter Abelard had been condemned as a heretic only a century earlier for moderate nominalism. Now the full Aristotelian corpus was available, further arming the advocates of persistent reason. Viewed in this context, Aquinas's harmonizing skills appear more significant.

Do these skills apply equally to his treatment of the virtues? There seems little of substantive importance beyond the expert cataloging and the generous inclusion of Aristotle's concept of the virtues as dispositions to the formation of character, guided by reason. The theological virtues are strongly presented, but Thomas's mission is basically to assert their superiority in the hierarchical rankings. The virtue of love, of course, both for the divine and for one's fellow man, is a breakthrough of the first magnitude in the history of morality. We must look to others for more objective and philosophical treatment of this virtue than is possible from Thomas. For all his great talent and confidence, he writes from an essentially closed view of the world.

3 Rousseau and the Republic of Virtue

The shift in emphasis from the virtues to virtue illustrates an instance of major usurpation of values in modern history, that of the Revolution in France. No longer are we dealing with Aristotle's technique for internalizing or socializing our characters towards virtuous conduct resulting in personal excellence and a state of flourishing as individuals and citizens. Nor are we dealing with the transcending personal virtues of Christianity that Aquinas stitched to the Aristotelian, headed by the matchless virtue of *caritas*, or love, the apotheosis of the Golden Rule of reciprocity bequeathed by the Judeo-Christian tradition as a measure of good conduct. Instead we are dealing with virtue as a social goal or standard, adapted first to justify the innovative ideas of a virtue-obsessed, talented writer, and later, unforgivably, to justify the Terrorism of the French Revolution.

On the theory that each age writes its own history of cataclysmic events like the Revolution, a post-Holocaust view tends to confirm Edmund Burke's judgment that the raising of the flag of liberty was fatally tarnished by excessive revenge and bloodshed. Similarly for an inquiry concerning the virtues, it is not just a matter of exposing the virtue concept as a mask or semblance in the service of partisan politics during the Revolution. Our memories include chilling footage of Third Reich adults and children marching in great parades, suffused with martial virtues, the whole panoply supporting a nation of virtue, cleansed of vice. The comparison is valid only for the dark underside of the Revolution, but such excesses are now viewed differently.

The inspiration and unsuspecting prophet for the Republic of Virtue, to which we will return, was Jean-Jacques Rousseau (1712–1778), an exceptional man by all accounts. Though he died well before the Revolution, his writings were essential to its ideology, and his influence on Robespierre, the ultimate Terrorist, absolute and critical. On balance, in spite of his bizarre personal history, Rousseau produced some of the most innovative and comprehensive secular social criticism formulated by his time. As often happens, his positions have been simplified by popular summarizing: the return to nature, the noble savage (a term he never used), the priority of feelings over reason, society's corruption of man, society's abuse of power, and the priority of the common good over individual aspirations. It is true that the transformation of his civic virtue concept into a gigantic propaganda mechanism by prominent architects of the Revolution was an unintended consequence, so far as Rousseau was concerned. The fact remains that without Rousseau there would have been no Republic of Virtue presiding as epiphany over the worst days of the Terror.

* * *

Our inquiry will focus on two aspects of Rousseau. First, the concept of public virtue in his value system, with particular attention to his development of the 'general will', and second, the creation, during the Revolutionary mania, of the 'Republic of Virtue' in his image.

Imagine a propertyless, self-educated, quarrelsome, eccentric vagrant, migrating from Geneva, his birthplace, through Italy and France, engaging in a series of random jobs and protective liaisons. Back in Paris in 1744, he formed a relationship with the servant girl in his lodgings and in time abandoned all five of their children to foundling hospitals, never to see them again, rather than face the responsibilities of parenthood. He eventually married the mother in 1768.

His portrait of the Paris period shows an uncommonly striking face. His intelligence apparently won him distinguished friends such as the young philosopher and encyclopedist Diderot. In 1749, age 37, this man of no particular achievement, although he was an accomplished musicologist, entered a contest sponsored by the Academy at Dijon for the best answer to the question of whether the restoration of the arts and sciences contributed to the purity of morals. Writing with intense passion on the side of morality, while constantly digressing along the lines that would become his hallmark, that man is naturally good but society and its institutions unfailingly debilitate this goodness, Rousseau struck a nerve among the academic judges, won first prize and soon became a celebrity.

The boldness of Rousseau's anti-progress stance in his *Discourse on the arts and sciences* should not be underestimated. This was the period of Adam Smith's *The Wealth of Nations* (1776), wherein material progress through technology was seen as mankind's new blessing. A major component of this technology, the efficiency derived from the division of labor, would be acknowledged by Smith as inspired in part by the pin factory so meticulously illustrated and described in the *Encyclopédie* of Rousseau's friend Diderot.

Though patronized by Diderot and his circle of *philosophes*, and later given refuge in England by Hume, Rousseau firmly rejected Enlightenment philosophy, particularly its accommodation with the rising class of capitalist entrepreneurs offering progress and reform. An intuitive populist, Rousseau identified himself with the ordinary and the powerless. His mission was to expose the power relationships through which the rich and their controlled institutions kept this constituency in a state of subordination, and to propose how this condition might be overthrown, or at the very least, rectified.

In this role, Rousseau continued to provoke the Establishment and outdistance the relatively benign censors of the Parlement of Paris and of the doomed Bourbon monarchy. His additional *Discourses* on social inequality, and on ways to minimize the injustices flowing from such inequality, secured his fame and prepared him for the two major works of his maturity, *Émile* and *The Social Contract*, both appearing in 1762. *Émile*, in the form of a philosophical novel, is basically an anti-clerical (though not anti-religious) tract, and a treatise on education and child-rearing by the hapless father. The *Contract* is a work of major importance in the history of social ideas but of less importance politically, despite its title.

The 'contract' idea has lineage extending back to Plato's *Republic* and beyond to the religious covenants of the Hebrew Bible. Suffice to note that Hobbes, considered in both England and France the leading philosopher of his time, had published in his *Leviathan* (1651), the warning that life would be 'solitary, poor, nasty, brutish and short' without the transition from a state of nature to a state of civilized government by way of an implied agreement or contract. Locke, in his *Second Treatise on Government* (1690), differed from Hobbes on the role of the governing sovereign, wishing to limit rather than amplify his powers, and he did not see nature so adversely. Yet government had an important role for Locke where natural conditions were deficient, and again the notion of contract, and its corollary, consent, were utilized. Rousseau, a voracious reader since childhood, was knowledgeable about Hobbes and Locke, having read them and additional philosophers, both secular and theological, in the library of his first benefactress, Mme de Warens. Moreover, history had brought contract theory into focus as never before, providing justification for the abrogation of obedience to authority on the part of Cromwell's Army, the Puritan dissenters, and the American colonists.

In this context, Rousseau's approach to contract is a distinct departure from the practical political emphasis of Hobbes and Locke. The contract should be a voluntary agreement that binds men together for a purpose, but not to escape from nature, nor from dangerous prepolitical conditions. Instead it is a device to restore man's social relations to those existing in an alleged virtuous, less civilized past, typically Republican Rome, or better, Sparta, with its superior austerity and resolve. The goal is beneficent enough: above all, the eradication of inequality, since that is the source of power in the hands of the few, and thus the source of injustice and the loss of freedom itself. The language is alternately inflammatory and seductive. The *Contract* opens with the words 'Man was born free and he is everywhere in chains,' but Rousseau has a sense of limits. Nowhere does he advocate revolution for existing societies, and his equality might conceivably translate into the minimal inequality of John Rawls, a modern contractarian, whom we will meet in Chapter 8. It is the means for attaining Rousseau's 'reign of virtue', his Utopia of the past, as outlined in the *Social Contract* and its complement, *Émile*, which make it morally repugnant for non-Rousseauvians.

Taking the text at face value, the state would consist of virtuous citizens, conditioned for that role from childhood through an educational process from our view perilously close to brain-washing. Aristotle's openly arrived at 'dispositions to character', using the virtues as models, guided by reason, are not for young Émile. 'Let him always believe he is the master but let it always really be you. There is no subjection so perfect as the one which retains the appearance of liberty; thus one captivates the very will itself.'[5] The citizen who refuses to place the conservation of the state above his own interests must perish, 'and when the guilty man is put to death it is less as a citizen than as an enemy.'[6] Add to these dismal recommendations an equally suspect dismissal of bureaucratic safeguards: 'Virtue is the only efficacious instrument. Therefore give up account books and papers and put finances in faithful hands; that is the only way to insure faithful administration.'[7] Particularly offensive is Rousseau's treatment of women in the *Contract* and *Émile*, considering that he flourished in their company and was constantly adored and supported by them. *Émile* is unremittingly patriarchal, with women educated only for a role of dependency. Restricted to caring for their families and households, they would be unable to 'tyrannize men' through their sexuality.[8] Inasmuch as a surge of feminism in eighteenth-century France was well on its way, in terms of both philosophical advocacy and high-level performance, Rousseau's continued appeal to women after publication of these books is all the more remarkable.

Selecting subjectively from a body of work is a risky enterprise when dealing with values and ideas. Additionally, world-views change, so that little is gained, for example, by dwelling on the severe class stratifications and other anomalies that might similarly be said to mar a legacy so revered as Plato's *Republic*. Still, Rousseau belongs to modern history. He is a contemporary not only of Enlightenment philosophers on the Continent, but of Adams, Jefferson, Madison and Franklin. These men also looked backward to Republican Rome for models of civic virtue. Madison, along with Hamilton and Jay, wrote the *Federalist Papers* (1787–88), in support of ratifying the Constitution, under the collective name of Publius, reflecting this grounding. Checks and balances on the departments of government, not bookkeeping angels, were among their prescriptions for the state. Franklin, like Adams, represented the sober virtues of the religious dissenters' tradition, but he was a colorful man as well. As emissary to France in late 1776, he helped win recognition for the new American republic. He also posed, like Rousseau, as a fur-capped, rustic sage and captivated the salons, but his performance was an exercise of diplomacy as well as enjoyment, devoid of cultism.[9]

On the positive side, there is the foe of injustice who finally fled France, saw his books burned in Geneva, suffered physically and mentally, yet maintained his convictions to the end. Judith Shklar, a Rousseauvian specialist, looks beyond the posturing and self-identification with virtue in his writings. She sees an underlying Rousseau who held, like Proudhon, 'that the social contract involved not government but the whole social and moral environment in which people might live decent and satisfying lives.'[10] His attacks on inequality, on subjugation, and particularly his concept of a benign general will are for her theoretical accomplishments of the first order, though she does not necessarily agree with his conclusions.

Rousseau's general will concept, which history ineluctably associates with him, is innovative, a change from previous will concepts that had been primarily theological and applicable to the individual's moral intentions from Augustine onward.[11] Rousseau ingeniously advances as a model the individual will functioning as a behavioral or psychological faculty to keep the passions in check. He does this much as Aristotle had assigned a similar guiding role for the making of individual, right choices, to reason and the virtues. For Rousseau, however, it is society and its conspiring institutions that are in effect a social disease requiring a collective social cure. What 'men in general' need, the *Social Contract* states, is a 'general will' to protect them against the general social and emotional forces that tend to victimize them by maintenance of inequality and thus deprivation of liberty. This countervailing, populist power is not associated in the *Contract* with any preferred type of government or economic system, though democracy is the least-favored.[12] One then might expect such a just general will to be associated in theory with some universal standard, such as the Stoics' brotherhood of man, or a Kantian Golden Rule, suitable for the anti-clerical Rousseau. Typically, Rousseau's eccentricities prevail. His particularisms approach the xenophobic. The locale of the state is preferably an agrarian, isolated, patriotic republic of the past. The important branch of government is the legislative, in the hands of a 'great legislator', such as Lycurgus or Moses. The Legislator will derive his anti-institutional power from the general will of the populace for his modest legislative duties, once the conditioning process among the citizens has taken root. In effect, as Shklar agrees, Rousseau's opposition to organized society and his theory of minimal government among mutually agreeing small groups, find their closest political analogue in classical anarchism.[13]

* * *

Rousseau's myth of virtue flourished in pre-Revolutionary France. A regime of luxury and greed, supported by a church regarded as venal and hypocritical, could hardly withstand such a rallying point for the venting of anger and demonstration of moral superiority. Journals reported pilgrimages to Ermenonville, the scene of his death, by the humble and the great, including Queen Marie-Antoinette and her royal children. Songs and plays about the philosopher proliferated. One collection of songs in his honor, for the benefit of an orphans' fund, included Franklin among its subscribers. Mme de Staël, the influential daughter of Necker, Louis XVI's finance minister, rhapsodized about his passion for virtue and morality in a letter published on the eve of the Revolution. After the second volume of his autobiographical *Confessions* appeared in 1789, Mercier, a contemporary historian, proclaimed him a primary 'author of the Revolution'. He credited Rousseau with endowing France with a concept of 'public virtue', replacing feudal concepts such as honor, with its outmoded standards of egoism and duelling.[14] By December 1791, the new National Assembly had voted to erect a statue of Rousseau and award a pension to his faithful wife, Thérèse Levasseur.

So far, no harm, but soon the beneficiaries squandered their inheritance. It will suffice to concentrate on one of his followers, Maximilien Robespierre, who completely fused his personality in the cloak of Rousseau's virtue, both as public figure and as an individual. Beheaded at age 36 after a political life involving the entire Revolution, Robespierre authored works comprising eight volumes, mostly political texts. They contain ample references to Rousseau as a model and source of 'divine' inspiration for the young lawyer. Like Rousseau, he believed in the mystic body of the people, and he saw himself as an embodiment of the Legislator in the *Social Contract*. It was only a short step for Robespierre, in the waning days of the Revolution, to strike terror in the hearts of the enemies of the state. The Reign of Terror, with which Robespierre is inevitably associated, was a wartime dictatorship during a period of national emergency (1793–94). Louis XVI had already been guillotined on January 21, 1793, condemned by a bare majority in a Convention overwhelmed by the oratory of another Rousseauvian, the 25-year old Louis de Saint-Just. Now to suppress internal dissension and prosecute France's foreign wars, a 10-member, Paris-based Committee on Public Safety, with Robespierre dominating, was empowered. In June 1794, the collaborating Revolutionary Tribunal was authorized to decree the death penalty, and executions accelerated. In the scramble to avoid inclusion in the bloody list, the Convention combined with Robespierre's enemies on the Committee. On July 27, 1794 he was arrested and on the next day guillotined. Saint-Just, also a member of the Committee, met a similar fate.

There still remains Rousseau's apotheosis in pageantry, the Festival of the Supreme Being on June 8, 1794, and prescription, the Law of 22 prairial (June 10, 1794), both shepherded by Robespierre. The Festival celebrated Rousseauvian ideas of a Republic of Virtue, bonded in patriotic rites to a Deist conception appropriate for a free

45

people. Superintended by David, the painter who would later transfer his talents to Napoleon, a half-million Parisians took part in the spectacle. Prints show an artificial mountain constructed in the Tuileries, in which thousands watch liberty-capped citizens lead an ox-driven carriage, mounted by an unattended, cap-waving *citoyenne*, to its entrance. The prescription, only two days later, is the infamous 'enemies of the people' legislation for the Revolutionary Tribunal, which swept away all pretense of rights for the accused, and finally netted its sponsors.

* * *

In this and the preceding chapter, we have analyzed virtue as an analogue of personal behavior. It is a building block on the way to the moral limitations of capitalism, which has been identified as a concern of the 'social justice' philosophers, such as Posner and Rawls, rather than the 'ethics' philosophers one usually meets in discussions of personal behavior.

In personal behavior, people seek standards or values to live by, and they seek maxims or rules of conduct to fortify or internalize these standards.[15] From the comparisons of theories of personal ethics in the first two chapters, it appears there are two broad divisions, equally compelling in regard to goals and justification. First, a pluralist, moderately relativist view, grounded in the concrete experience of everyday life, whose supporters claim to be 'Aristotelian'; second, a more abstract, absolute basis for morality, grounded in obligation, whose supporters claim to be 'Kantian'. A third view, utilitarianism, is concerned with results more than an end goal of being, or feeling, good, but when adjusted for some moral complement, say benevolence, is very close to modern social and political life, and should be included. Utilitarianism is nearer to the relative than the absolute. My own bias, as is probably clear, is for the Aristotelian, in my search for a more socially-just capitalism.

The virtue concept was chosen for the analogue because of its practical use in theory (the Aristotelian technique) and because its extended use over time illustrates the inevitable impact of cultural change on moral theory.[16] It also illustrates the dangers of moral purity

46

or absolutism. The great question about personal behavior, of course, is to what extent such behavior, and not external causation, such as capitalism, is responsible for social ills. Asking the question, and thinking about it, is part of the answer.

Notes

1 See Lee H. Yearley, *Mencius and Aquinas: Theories of Virtue and Conceptions of Courage* (Albany, N.Y.: State University of New York Press, 1990). The author presents a comparative philosophical-theological analysis of courage between Meng Tzu (Mencius, 372–289 B.C.), an early Confucian, and Aquinas. Aside from Yearley's impressive analysis of their differing theoretical approaches and conceptual restraints, he finds real resemblances, particularly in relation to false courage (semblances) and the expansion of courage into the religious realm.

2 Simone Weil, 'The Iliad or the Poem of Force', in Stanley Hauerwas and Alasdair MacIntyre, eds., *Revisions* (Notre Dame: University of Notre Dame Press, 1983), 222–48.

3 *Ibid.*, 231.

4 Yearley, *Mencius and Aquinas*, 29.

5 Jean-Jacques Rousseau, *Émile* (Paris: Pléiade, published under direction of B. Gagnebin and M. Raymond, 1961, rep. 1969), vol. 4 of complete works, 363.

6 Jean-Jacques Rousseau, *The Social Contract* (London: Penguin, 1968, translated by Maurice Cranston), 79.

7 Jean-Jacques Rousseau, *Écrits politiques* (Paris: Pléiade, published under direction of B. Gagnebin and M. Raymond, 1961, rep. 1969), vol. 3 of complete works, 265–66.

8 Rousseau, *Émile*, 694.

9 Note should be taken of J.G.A. Pocock's claim that the American founders identified with Machiavellian and Rousseauvian concepts of republican virtue, emphasizing statecraft and public interest, and exemplified by models of personal virtue and public-good dedication, such as Cato and Cicero. Pocock, a highly-regarded historian of European intellectual

history, additionally claims traditional liberal analysis of the primacy of Locke's influence on the founders (self-interest, individualism, anti-statism and property rights) is historical 'myth'. J.G.A. Pocock, *The Machiavellian Moment: Florentine Political Thought and the Atlantic Republican Tradition* (Princeton: Princeton University Press, 1975), 506–09. For rebuttal, see John P. Diggins, *The Lost Soul of American Politics: Virtue, Self-Interest and the Foundations of Liberalism* (New York: Basic Books, 1984), 3–17, 366–67. Diggins in turn emphasizes the moral and religious elements in America's founding, repeated in Lincoln's agony.

10 Judith N. Shklar, 'General Will', *Dictionary of the History of Ideas*, ed. by Philip P. Wiener, (New York: Charles Scribner's Sons, 1973), vol. 2, 280.

11 See Patrick Riley, *The General Will before Rousseau: The Transformation of the Divine into the Civic* (Princeton: Princeton University Press, 1986). Riley acknowledges Shklar's eminence on Rousseau's general will and traces the preceding theological disputes relating to particular will among Pascal, Arnauld, Bayle, and Malebranche.

12 Rousseau, *The Social Contract*, 112.

13 Shklar, 'General Will', 280.

14 Carol Blum, *Rousseau and the Republic of Virtue* (Ithaca, N.Y.: Cornell University Press, 1986), 144. This is an exceptionally fine overview of Rousseau from a psychological and cultural perspective.

15 The most universal secular table of virtues now in force is the Law of the Boy Scouts: A Scout is Trustworthy, Loyal, Helpful, Friendly, Courteous, Kind, Obedient, Cheerful, Thrifty, Brave, Clean, and Reverent. These are basically the affective, or emotional, virtues of the good citizen, reflecting post-Victorian English society, in which Scouting was born, and in which personal conduct was of primary concern. Note the absence of the four cardinal virtues, although bravery approximates courage.

16 Russell Hardin, (see *supra* Chapter 1, n. 5), cautions me about the defensibility of Aristotelian virtue theory, on the view that it is insufficiently grounded on principles that allow us to deduce or justify it. The virtues are limited by cultural contexts and often conflict with one another. (Letter to the author of 28 July 1993.)

4 Capitalism and slavery: an analogue of institutional failure and redemption

1 The Pre-Columbian School for Slavery

In Chapter 1 we introduced a theory of capitalism claiming moral credentials, Judge Posner's 'wealth-maximizing' entry. In Chapters 2 and 3, we examined moral life in terms of western philosophy's most durable prescription for personal behavior, the concept of internalized, rationally-guided virtue, invented by Aristotle in response to Socrates' question: 'How should one live one's life?'

Posner's conservative theory of cost-efficient capitalism was identified as a 'social justice' theory, in harmony with the tradition that capitalism contains moral possibilities, as asserted by the father of capitalist theory, Adam Smith, in his *An Inquiry into the Nature and Causes of the Wealth of Nations* (1776). In this empirical, anecdotal work, Smith dealt mortal blows to all preceding command economies, as well as the reigning economic theory of his day, state-directed mercantilism, functioning both as monopoly-protector and instrument of economic warfare. It was Smith's passionate faith in the free-market system, as opposed to the encroaching, inefficient state, that made him the apostle of laissez-faire, subordinating Smith the moralist. It is my purpose in this book to question modern capitalism – not Smith's – about its morality quotient. In the final chapter, we will measure the American capitalist system against a standard of 'fairness', a less ambiguous word than 'morality' for such evaluation, but still a matter of moral accountability.

On that path we can sharpen our moral acuity by considering, in addition to the personal virtue analogue, two social justice analogues.

The first concerns the institutions confronting slavery in the American experience, in this chapter. The second concerns the delivery by institutions of constitutional social justice, in the following two chapters. The underlying logic is that personal virtue, while all to the good, ranks below the performance of social institutions – the courts, the Congress, the media, the church, the Presidency – in the matter of fairly allocating, or denying, our rights and economic resources.

Why use analogues? The analogue as instrument of argument has a time-honored pedigree. It is a more worldly version of venerated 'naively-wise' devices, such as the parable, the fable, and the allegory. It relates to the imaginative techniques of language itself, the metaphor, the simile, and the rhyme. Its emotional content helps us contend with the charge that reason alone, as the philosophers warn us, is inadequate when human hunger and dignity are on the line. In terms of social justice, who knows what fires were lit across Europe when some unknown plaintiff, contending with plagues and serfdom in the dark days of the fourteenth century, simply proclaimed:

> When Adam delved and Eve span,
> Who was then the gentleman?

The tropism between literary device and morality is further heightened when we note that great plays and novels invariably have some moral value. There are certainly alternate routes for ruminating about the moral limitations of capitalism, but a predilection for analogy need not be a disqualification.

* * *

In slavery we face mankind's most astounding sin, a moral aberration terminated in America only by our Thirteenth Amendment to the Constitution in 1865. It is futile to get to its heart in terms of sin and morality. No medieval list of sins, no Decalogue or Testament, no serenely rational Aristotle or Jefferson declared slavery out of bounds. Its persistence, ancient and modern, rests on publicly-sanctioned economic preference.[1] Modern plantation slavery, the subject of this chapter, was clearly an economic issue, a preference to use coerced humans as the labor factor of production in order to make more money.

History confers two verdicts on capitalism in relation to modern slavery. First it failed morally through the very brilliance of its blind success. It not only produced an ocean-bound slave trade of immense quantity and logistics, but also ruthlessly converted the human cargo into a formidably profitable slave labor force, both endeavors lasting well over two hundred years. Neither Parliaments nor Constitution-makers, bishops nor judges, rich nor poor, could stem this process during its glory days of the eighteenth and nineteenth centuries. There is little point in conjuring a name for such an overwhelming alliance of politics, wealth, and sanctimony. 'Hegemony' is often used, but the conjuncture of the complex system was more fortuitous than planned. It was neither prescribed nor necessary for the success of mercant-ilism, capitalism, or for the wealth of nations. The basic motivation was the untrammeled profit motive, and for this the infant, unregu-lated, still-unnamed system for producing and allocating economic resources draws the lion's share of blame. Assigning blame is one of morality's intrinsic flaws, but recall Lincoln, the reluctant Emancip-ator, agonizing: 'If anything is wrong, then slavery is wrong.' Against contending claims of politics and interest, only principle remained.

The second verdict conferred on capitalism as an institution is one of success for its essential role in abolishing the slavery it helped create, at a high peak of the system's economic value to the British empire as well as to its European competitors, in 1833. Three decades later, capitalism exercised a similar role for the American Union. The English abolitionists, of course, were not elite capitalists, although men like Josiah Wedgwood, of pottery fame, were early stalwarts against their class interests.[2] In turn, Calvinist-capitalist New England became the very heart of abolition support. Additionally, the institu-tion of capitalism invoked an implicit understanding of free labor as a component of the free market system, a vision logically inconsistent with forced labor, as Adam Smith noted.[3] Capitalism's unwritten theory added thereby a moral dimension to its free market foundation.

In this respect, the rise and fall of Atlantic slavery cannot be under-stood without examining English precedents. Our Civil War, with its 600,000 dead and continuing racial consequences, suggests otherwise,

51

but Anglo-American slavery is best comprehended in sequence, particularly in relation to the role of capitalism. In summary, capitalism, like Christianity and the prevailing concept of human progress itself, was first dishonored and then redeemed in its confrontation with slavery. David Brion Davis, our most distinguished historian of modern slavery, makes the point brilliantly in relation to Christianity and progress.[4] Seymour Drescher, a ranking luminary in the immensely rich historiography of slavery, can be drafted for a similar claim for capitalism's redemption, especially in the prototype British experience.[5]

* * *

Capitalism comes sharply into focus in the slavery analogue. We can start with Europe's awakening from its retrograde days of feudalism, malnutrition, inclement weather, and isolation. This so-called 'Rise of the West' led inexorably to the massive pillaging of African natives. In fact the story of Atlantic slavery begins with the revival of the ancient Mediterranean slave trade that accompanied the demographic and commercial expansion of early modern Europe.

This awakening, from the tenth century onward, was marked by an increase in productivity that accelerated a remarkable growth in population. The best estimates are that Europe, including the Byzantine Empire and Russia north of the Black Sea, increased from a base of 30 million to 40 million in the two centuries from 1000 to 1200.[6] The agricultural revolution itself was phenomenal, involving massive deforestation to increase arable land, and the introduction of the moldboard plow, a complex piece of machinery able to cut, breach and turn the furrow. Attached to a pair of wheels and drawn by multiple teams of oxen, the plow enabled the lords of the manor to organize peasant-serfs into group labor forces able to cultivate long strips of land. A turn from two-field crop rotation, the classical rule of the vast Roman slave-based agricultural system, to a three-field system, allowing one field to lie fallow, added spring planting to the cycle. This more than doubled cultivation on the same land, while adding spring crops – the oats, peas and beans, rich in carbohydrates – that nourished the burgeoning population. These steps were turning points in man's mastery of nature. Lynn White, Jr., our foremost historian of medieval technology, regarded the new heavy plow as the changing force from bare subsistence farming to farming limited only by the equipment's use:

> No more fundamental change in the idea of man's relation to the soil can be imagined: once man had been part of nature; now he became her exploiter.[7]

Man as exploiter responded with similar advances in non-agricultural technology. These were the heady days of proto-capitalism, long before the social power and significance of the system were comprehended. Invention, trade, finance and risk-taking shared in the burst of energy. The manorial agricultural surplus enabled feudal castle refugees, travelling traders, and adventurers to form hundreds of new walled towns. Here the 'free air" drew craftsmen, artists, technicians, merchants and power-brokers. Emulating the capacity for organization demonstrated in agriculture, the towns-people and their militant leaders established craft guilds, built arsenals, ships, factories, town halls and cathedrals, all elements of civic pride, fed by ambition and competition.

The Italian city-states, cradled in the Mediterranean and sea-going by environment and tradition, took the lead in Europe's financial and trading rebirth. Freed from Muslim domination of their sea-lanes, communes like Venice and Genoa became formidable nautical competitors, creating oligarchical republics wherein merit and daring could lead to wealth and political power. The merchant-minded Venetians excelled in maritime technology. Perfecting the mariner's compass, along with the traverse table and sea charts, they created the art of dead-reckoning. The effect was to open up the Mediterranean, by the thirteenth century, to transportation during the overcast months of October to April, doubling the sea-time and productivity of their great investment in ship-building. Maritime insurance, collective syndicates for raising funds, new credit instruments such as bills of exchange, and the art of double-entry bookkeeping hastened the acquisitive process. The Venetian doges, in effect merchant princes, cut their eye teeth on the relentless Arab raids preceding the Iberian reconquest of the Mediterranean. Combining diplomacy with sea power, they captured the Byzantine market and became the pivot of exotic trade flowing overland through the Alps to northern Europe, whose somnolent, war-ravaged countries would eventually succeed the Italian city-states as centers of early capitalism. Meanwhile, between four wars with Genoa, the calculating Venetians seized upon the Crusades as a commercial opportunity. Contracting with Popes and naive knights, they built prodigious fleets for transporting the warriors of the Fourth Crusade and their giant horses to the Holy Land. En route, they argued over payment, abandoned the quest and instead conquered and looted Christian Constantinople for themselves in 1204.[8]

Slavery was just another bookkeeping item for the builders of St. Mark's Cathedral, now ablaze with the four bronze horses, masterpieces of Roman sculpture, transported as trophies from the hippodrome at Constantinople. Between 1414 and 1423, records indicate about 10,000 slaves, mostly female, were sold in Venice alone. The Florentines declared open house for the importation of slaves in 1543, including any Byzantine Christians that might be offered.[9]

There is a theory that slavery diminishes in direct proportion to excessive 'free labor' alternates, that it does not pay to capture, feed and dominate slaves when the non-servile force is available at subsistence wages. Emphasizing elements of slaveholder paternalism and efficiency, a respected school of modern historiography balances out the profit statement with a contrary conclusion, notably for the American antebellum South. It claims plantation records show that slavery, organized under capitalist principles, was a profitable choice over free labor.[10] This assertion, though challenged, reminds us of the moral and historical ambiguities we face with slavery as an institution, and certainly of its immense variations over time and location. The traditional high-cost theory, however, helps explain the gradual dissolution of Roman slavery, at its height representing approximately thirty-five per cent of the city of Rome's population.[11] As the decadent Empire disintegrated over the centuries, it created its own underclass of serfs and peasants, discriminated against both legally and economically, making slavery unnecessary.[12]

Consider the Black Death plague of the 1340s, accompanied by war and famine, that reduced the European population of 80 million by at least one-third, according to reliable demographers. Would not the reduced labor force conversely produce a significant turn to slavery? A modest increase was experienced in the Mediterranean area, but no more than that in such a distressed, static period. Only when European vitality, fired by the same novel desire for gain evidenced in the pre-plague agricultural and technological revolutions, revived dynamically, did slavery accelerate. This irresistible vitality, which restored the population to its former figures in about 130 years, or five generations, set the stage for a new round of economic expansion. This round would be accelerated exponentially by the New World discoveries of the fifteenth and sixteenth centuries, with their resulting flood of slave-mined silver coinage reinforcing the insatiable profit motive. The double-edged confluence of progress and human misery would become explosive by the nineteenth century and would eventually lead to America's tragic war.

The Mediterranean school for slavery continued even after the Ottoman reconquest of Constantinople in 1453. Shut off from their Black Sea and Balkan markets, the Italians turned to negotiating with sub-Saharan Arab slave caravans, which were already bringing thousands of blacks to the shores of Libya, destined for Arab lands or for the highest bidder. The new commerce established a fateful entry into black slavery on the part of the Europeans.

Unlike the predominantly white, mostly Slavic household slaves previously sold in Italy, where a labor shortage for this class persisted in spite of the fourteenth-century calamities, the new black captives were recruited for vineyards and sugar plantations, mainly in Sicily, Cyprus, Crete and Majorca. The chastened Crusaders had learned the art of sugar cultivation on their plantations in the Levant, their products being financed and transported to Europe by Italian bankers and merchants. The new substitute for honey, used originally for medicinal purposes as well as sweetener, would come into world prominence when more affluent consumers demanded it insatiably for their drinks and condiments.

The Mediterranean laboratory for Atlantic black plantation slavery was now complete. Its experts were skilled in the warfare, colonizing, transportation, trading, and financing of slavery, and were aided by the consensual suspension of morality necessary to coerce humans to supply whatever mass consumer market paid best.

2 Atlantic Slavery Begins

Empire and discovery now dominate the history of Atlantic slavery, with a central role for Portugal, then only one million strong, jutting into the Atlantic, its harbors ideally situated for Italian merchant ships bearing goods from the East, destined for England and Western Europe. The paradigm for sea-struck royalty is Henry, the Navigator Prince (1394–1460), basking in the Christian reconquest of his country from the infidel Muslims. Henry dedicated himself to gain and Christianizing the heathen across the oceans and down the west coast of Africa, the latter a strategy for outwitting Arab caravans in the search for gold in the largely unknown continent.

Fortified by Genoese naval technology and capital, Henry established a naval arsenal, an observatory and a center for the study of geography and navigation. Feats of navigation by Portuguese seamen in the fifteenth and sixteenth centuries were spectacular, memorized by schoolchildren thereafter: Diaz, first to round the Cape of Good Hope (1488); Vasco da Gama, around the Cape and on to India (1497–98); Cabral (1501), returning to Lisbon in triumph from India, laden with spices, casually claiming possession of immense Brazil on the first leg of his journey; Magellan, under the Spanish flag, circumnavigating the world (1519–22), proving the roundness of the earth and giving map-makers a relatively accurate idea of the world's water and land areas. In their brief century of eminence, before yielding to England, Spain, France and Holland, the Portuguese created an empire extending from Brazil to the Moluccas in the East Indies, the main source of Arab wealth in spices. There are magnificent Japanese screens on view in western museums memorializing the visits of these merchant-conquerors, long-nosed, top-hatted, wearing Elizabethan-type pantaloons, with black slaves holding their parasols.

It was in the period before Columbus' navigations that Portuguese sugar and slavery served as precursors to New World slavery and to New World wealth. Over thirty voyages probed the African west coast in the 1440s, resulting in trading establishments on the offshore islands of Madeira, near the Azores, and São Tomé, much further south, below the continental bulge. By the 1490s Madeira had become a flourishing sugar colony, manned by black slaves. Its production exceeded that of the entire Mediterranean plantation system, including the Crusaders', and was shipped directly to Antwerp. A jewel of the Spanish crown, Antwerp was a major entry port for Portuguese spices from Asia as well as Atlantic sugar. In turn, Antwerp re-shipped copper from the technologically-advanced German mines, providing a medium of exchange for acquiring black slaves. The medium was as tawdry as the business itself. It would be supplemented by rum, rifles, low-grade tobacco and manufactured cloths and articles over the next three centuries.

* * *

Columbus spent ten pre-voyage years on Madeira, making some excursions but mainly representing Genoese sugar buyers. We can no longer categorize this complex, once universally adulated man, as a master mariner achieving gain and fame, against insuperable odds, through discovery of a westward and presumably shorter route to the fabulous 'Indies'. A cascade of books exploring the man as well as his mission has de-mythologized the driven sailor. Scholars praising Columbus before censuring him as a symbol of imperialist marauding caution us to see him in the context of his times. His modest lineage fueled an ambition to rise socially in one of the few areas available for a Renaissance outsider, to enrich his king in order to enrich and ennoble himself. The long years of flattering and promotion in the royal courts of Portugal and Spain were tactical dues paid in a system of courtiers competing for sponsorship. Throughout Europe artists and writers as well as explorers tempered their newly-found 'individualism' with such activity.

Exploration was above all a royal business priority, sanctioned by a religious zeal for conversion and made possible by the great commercial and technological expansion of the recent centuries. The commercial aspect allowed Columbus to negotiate the business-like contract, so important to the future realm of capitalism, in which he

57

stipulated a grandiose title and a stake in his discoveries commensurate with the mercantilist gold, spices and empire his contractors coveted. The religious side, in essence the moral ingredient of the age of exploration, was easily accommodated. Columbus was given to apocalyptic visions and believed he was God's instrument. He was a devotee of Biblical revelation, including information in the book of Esdras that the earth was six-sevenths part land and one-seventh water, enabling him to chart the Indies of Asia in the vicinity of San Salvador. Ferdinand and Isabella need no certification for their piety. Having conquered and expelled the infidel Muslims, they turned on their eminent Jewish community, expelling any non-converted cargo against a deadline of July 1, 1492, a month and two days before Columbus departed for what turned out to be the New World.

* * *

Columbus as disputed symbol also serves as model for the Eurocentric explorer-invader who perceives aliens as inferiors personally and culturally, a stance inevitably allied with racism. Like an imperialist Prospero, he 'discovers' lands whose inhabitants might feel already discovered, since they are there. Invoking magical powers, he confers new religious names, a theological one for Trinidad, and eponymous saints for other islands. These are now considered exercises in deracination and alienation, in line with the basic strategies of enslavement enumerated by Harvard's sociologist Orlando Patterson, an authority on slavery in world history.[13]

Culturally, the doomed Tainos and other natives are thought to be seen by Columbus as prelapsal anachronisms, curiously naked, without any significant crafts or traditions, people not to be understood anthropologically but to be utilized and converted. Columbus himself was not a slaver, although the records indicate he was immersed in the reigning ideology and ready to impose slavery on native prisoners, had he not more pressing problems. His second expedition in 1493 was a major undertaking, involving seventeen caravels and 1,500 white colonists, hoping to find gold or to become landowners, artisans and possibly sugar planters in the balmy, fruitful islands he had propagandized. Suffice to say Columbus proved to be a poor administrator, returning in defeat to Spain, where he incredibly recouped his prestige and mounted still two additional, wide-ranging voyages. Perhaps this is the basic Columbus after all, a supremely obsessed, pragmatically modern mariner, pleasing to any Yankee skipper, the Admiral of the Ocean Seas described by the historian Samuel Eliot Morison. Certainly, his cultural myopia is the weakest of charges to level against Columbus. The eminence of pre-Columbian art and culture is a belated discovery. We are reminded that the rationalists of the Enlightenment generally dismissed Gothic architecture as savage, and only a few like Picasso perceived early in the present century the imagination and authenticity of African art.

Recall also the dissenters to the prevailing ideology. If we believe in an optimistic theory of progress, such as one supporting capitalism's redemption in the matter of slavery, we need not accept history as determined, beyond the reach of unique individuals. The moral prophets are heard over time – generally too long a time – undermining official wisdom through the force of ideas, the antecedents of counteraction. The candidate often opposed to the Iberian archetype is Bartolemé de las Casas (1474–1566).

Las Casas used his ninety-two years of life to make a major contribution to the social justice of the sixteenth century. A scholar, historian and advocate for the Indians in the Council of the Indies in Madrid, he was also a devotee of Columbus. His *Book of the First Navigation*, started about forty years after Columbus, and based on a copy of Columbus' lost original log, is the primary source for this voyage.[14] It probably was prepared in connection with the thirty years spent in producing Las Casas' *History of the Indies*, which he cautiously stipulated could be published only posthumously. In it he describes and denounces the oppression and injustice the Europeans were inflicting on their colonial peoples. His open-mindedness to other cultures and his analysis of the underlying motivation of unconscionable enrichment were pathbreaking. Las Casas had undeniable credentials. As a young priest, he took part in the harsh conquest of Cuba and was rewarded with a royal land-grant including an allotment of Indian serfs. After twelve years of participation in the conquest of the Caribbean, he renounced his serfs and returned to Spain to plead for their better treatment. For the rest of his life, he voyaged back and forth, propagandizing his cause with petitions and sermons. Gaining the favor of the emperor Charles V, he obtained legislation restricting Indian serfdom to manumission after a single generation of ownership, an early instance of the moral ambiguity of modern slavery, that is, the alternation of the promise and the whip. The colonial interests, including opposition churchmen, managed to sabotage this modest gain, eluding the bureaucrats in the over-burdened Escorial, but Las Casas pressed on steadfastly in the Council with public letters and debates. In a famous debate in 1550 at the theological Council of Valladolid, he rebutted the leading court scholar, who cited Aristotle's unfortunate remarks on slavery to justify the 'just war' against the Indians. The omnipresent Aristotle, however, whom we have noted as central to the concept of personal virtue in the preceding chapter, would not be resurrected by advocates of slavery in England and in the southern American states in the 1800s. The seeds of Las Casas' message were apparently great, spreading beyond Spain. There were of course others speaking out in the sixteenth century. Michel de Montaigne (1533–92), the French politician and essayist, who thought cruelty, because of its premeditation, the worst of vices,[15] deplored the 'millions of harmless people... massacred, ravaged and put to the sword... for the traffic of pearls and pepper.'[16] The sea-change in thought, however, was far on the horizon. In 1645, John Winthrop, governor of the Massachusetts Bay Colony, received a proposal from his colonist brother-in-law, pleading for a war against the Narragansetts, so that the captives could be exchanged for West Indian black slaves, 'for I do not see how we can thrive until we get into a stock of slaves sufficient to do all our business...'[17] In this perspective, Las Casas is an antecedent of Granville Sharp, Thomas Clarkson and William Wilberforce, the successful abolitionist leaders of nineteenth-century England.

* * *

Before leaving early Atlantic slavery and entering the eighteenth and nineteenth centuries wherein black plantation slavery rose and fell, attention should be paid to the largely Spanish depredations of the sixteenth and seventeenth centuries, involving the Amerindians. The dismal costs must be tallied, if only to make sure they are not forgotten.

The walls of the Mexican muralists – Rivera, Orozco and Siquieros – tell it all: the conquistadores with their furious swords, crosses, riflefire and strange new horses intimidating and destroying great civilizations. These were not just buccaneering expeditions. Some 240,000 men and women, including artisans and professionals, emigrated from Spain alone to America's continents and islands in the sixteenth century.[18] These emigrants, with their so-called *hidalgo* mentality, though courageous and versatile, were not disposed to hard labor when the indigenous population could be coerced accordingly.

Gold and silver – and later, ranchland – were the primary objectives of mainland Spanish emigration and domination. In the wake of Cortés' conquest of Central Mexico (1520s) and Pissaro's of Inca Peru (early 1530s), a rush of emigrants made these countries the centers of Spanish New World population. Immensely productive silver mines in both regions made silver the chief export to Spain. Potosi, in Upper Peru, became the world's largest source of silver for a hundred years before the mines were exhausted in the 1640s. The military conquests, the forced labor, and to a much larger degree the European diseases visited upon the non-immunized Amerindians, were devastating. Statistics accepted by leading scholars tell us that the population of pre-Spanish Central Mexico fell from over 25 million to 1.9 million in 1585, less than seventy years. Earlier the Spanish had made Hispaniola (now Haiti and the Dominican Republic) the advance base for their colonizing operations. By the 1520s, less than thirty years later, the Arawak natives, like Columbus' Tainos, were extinct, victims of disease, mass murder and oppressive labor.[19]

Moralists may ask what manner of men were agents for this genocide, quite apart from the unintended carrying of disease. Sixteenth-century Spain, defender of the faith, was the envy of Europe. Her armed forces were supreme, her Armada kept Shakespeare's England in a state of terror. There were cracks in the regime: men like Las Casas, Cervantes and El Greco were dissenters in their own fashion from the official arrogance and punctilio. The crown avoided the ocean-going slave trade for various reasons and drew distinctions between chattel slavery and serfdom. Yet in one instance in Central

America, when the conquistadores received too little tribute, they branded Amerindians on the face and shipped over 50,000 to Panama, Peru and the Caribbean.[20]

An initial explanation rests in the school of slavery in which the European expansionists matriculated. The Mediterranean of piracy, plunder and cruelty – a 'theatre of horrors', in Orlando Patterson's phrase – was easily transferred to the Caribbean and on to the New World mainland, including Brazil and eventually New England, with its savaging of the Pequot Indians. Another causal entry rests on the dimensions of time and space in the world-view of four hundred years ago. The immense ocean, delaying information and news between the European core and the colonial periphery, diminished moral reaction – out of sight, out of mind. (Moral philosophers still comfort us with temporal and spatial absolution, offering terminology such as the 'robust zone of indifference' we need to insulate ourselves from distant calamities beyond control.)[21] There was the religious motive as well as the feigned horror of cannibalism, and for the blacks, outright racism. A final reason: the weight of the reigning capitalist ideology. To avoid the wealth and power available from the slave trade and the slave colonies would be, in David Brion Davis' words, 'almost as unthinkable as spurning nuclear technology in the world of today.'[22]

3 The Rise and Fall of Black Slavery

First, the magnitude of the Atlantic black slave trade should be reviewed, in order to understand its commercial significance and the difficulties facing abolitionists hoping to end such a powerful institution.

From Columbus' time through 1870, a total of 11.5 million slaves were imported from Africa to the New World. To narrow our focus, consider that 7.4 million were imported in the eighteenth century and a final 2.5 million in the nineteenth century.[23]

Further qualifications: in the eighteenth century, using figures now considered conservative, Brazil imported over two million slaves, accounting for the largest portion. The United States accounted for the smallest segment, less than 500,000. Yet at the break of the Civil War, Southern slaves amounted to over 3.8 million. By 1825, the United States had the largest proportion of slaves in the New World for a startling reason: their system successfully bred its own slaves, while the Caribbean and other systems constantly required new shipments for growth and replacement. The figures support the claims of care and paternalism in the United States, that is, a relative concern for the investment value of its slaves, measured by fertility. Additionally the self-generating increase demonstrates the formidable courage, resourcefulness and religiously-inspired solidarity of the slave families themselves.[24]

Regarding the slave trade, the founding fathers tempered their slave-permitting Constitution with a proviso that the country would cease engaging in the slave trade after twenty years from ratification, or 1808 (Article I, 9 [1]). As a result, slaveholders stepped up their activity as the deadline approached. Still, the trade was never a major consideration for the Southern states, compared with the fear of abolition. Practically all the Southern states supported the proviso against the trade at its inception.

The New World slaves were recruited almost entirely from the western coast of Africa, and mostly from the mid-continental Guinea coast region, extending for only about 200 miles inland, and from the Congo and Angolan region farther south. This small portion of Africa as geographical homeland has enabled historians to establish the disconcerting claim that African chieftains and rulers were thoroughly complicit in delivering their subjects to the white traders. Orlando Patterson, a black sociologist who has sifted the evidence, concludes that the 7.4 million slaves shipped from Africa in the eighteenth century were already prisoners of war from intra-African conflicts, or simply kidnapped in response to the awards offered by the cynical white traders. The distinction between actual wars and kidnapping being difficult, he concludes that 70 per cent were kidnapped.[25] In this respect, all who touched slavery had, in terms of Jean-Paul Sartre's metaphor for twentieth-century collaborators, *mains sales*.

This leads inevitably to comparison of Atlantic slavery with the Holocaust of World War II. No exoneration is available from such comparison, but both should be examined continually in order to be remembered. First, recall that at least 20 per cent of the slaves perished during the gathering, marching and shipping. This stark cost-factor affected the white seamen for approximately 13 per cent, a testimonial to the implacable allure of the profit motive. Second, figures 'by the century' need narrower focus to enable us to comprehend the logistics involved in the slow, wind-powered transatlantic trade, symbolized by the packed-deck sleeping-quarters diagrams that were to become abolitionist broadsides, hanging in homes throughout England and the American North. The trade averaged 750,000 per decade in the eighteenth century and 250,000 per decade from 1811–70.[26] By contrast, at least six million Jews and three to four other millions were destroyed systematically by the Germans in less than five years. There are no degrees of evil to be strained from this comparison. Capitalism escapes Holocaust charges, but its ally, the concept of progress so firmly demonstrated by David Brion Davis as abetting nineteenth-century abolition, lies in ashes.

4 Capitalism and Slavery

We turn now to some special pleading for capitalism in regard to slavery. It is not a matter of winning a debate, or of proving a case beyond doubt. Modern capitalism has survived for close to 300 years and will rise or fall by verdict of its marketplace arbiter, popular consent. It does not need anti-slavery credentials. Still the analogue as moral example requires fleshing out and will benefit from the dialectic of charge and countercharge.

In capitalism's favor, the broad background finds slavery suddenly capitulating in the same period in which the industrial revolution irrevocably seized the day, bringing capitalist, or so-called 'bourgeois', values into supremacy. Intuitively, a connection rests in this background.

Following the historians, and because we are interested in theory as instigator of action, we can start with Eric Williams' *Capitalism and Slavery*, which gained wide attention in the 1940s.[27] Briefly, Williams identified capitalism, much as this chapter has done, as a protean force, led by the profit motive, which organized and developed slavery into a worldwide economic institution. Others had acknowledged the awesome force of capitalism as agent of material progress, notably Karl Marx in the *Communist Manifesto* (1848), before exposing the reverse side that particularly interested them. For Williams, the reverse image was a conspiracy theory. The capitalists and their unwitting abolitionist allies ended West Indian slavery as the institution sharply declined in economic value to the Empire as a whole. The strategy also involved using abolition as a distraction from growing labor unrest in England itself. In other words, the capitalist governing class abolished slavery as an act of dubious euthanasia or damage control in order to placate free laborers who were beginning to see themselves as wage-slaves. Additionally, African enslavement was declared indispensable for developing the New World, and the capital amassed was alleged to have financed the industrial revolution.

Lending credence to this attack on capitalism, written in the tradition of materialist-determined history, is the unusual background of Williams himself (1911–81). A black native of Trinidad, he gained a PhD in history and political science at Oxford University in 1938, taught at Howard University in America, and eventually returned to Trinidad to become its first prime minister (1962–81), after the colony achieved independence from Britain. His moderate 'social capitalism' led Trinidad to become the wealthiest of the Caribbean nations, and his *Capitalism and Slavery* was only one of seven scholarly books on West Indian slavery. Had he written later, after American civil rights legislation and the rise of black studies, his thesis would have gained even more attention.

Conspiracy theories gain credibility through claims containing at least a grain of truth or coincidence. Seymour Drescher, an authority on British slavery, acknowledges that British slave-production of sugar, its West Indian specialty, became relatively level as the agitation against slavery mounted in the 1820s to 1840s. He produces strong evidence, however, to demonstrate that world-colonial sugar production, practically all slave-based, by Britain, Spain, France and other European countries, increased by about fifty per cent in this period.[28] At abolition time, British West Indian sugar still constituted a large and profitable segment of total British overseas trade, and also absorbed a significant portion of exports from the metropolis. In brief, world-slavery was enjoying a golden age of profit, with apparently unlimited financing from Europe, slaves from Africa, and entrepreneurs from the colonies. The situation entitled the nation of shop-keepers to a certain moral superiority from its withdrawal from the slave trade (1807), and then from the institution (1833).

British imperialist capitalism does not escape scot-free from charges of moral hypocrisy in the abolition process. As ruler of the seas, the Empire's naval attacks against other nations still in the trade were perceived to be a mercantilist ploy to maintain competitive equality. The United States succumbed to the paranoia about British 'philanthropy', becoming alarmed over exaggerated reports that slave-trade abolition by its two-time foe was an entering wedge to end slavery in still independent Texas, nearby Cuba and possibly the American South, even though the latter region, fortified by Eli Whitney's cotton gin (1793), accounted for seventy per cent of the cotton for Manchester looms. The charges of intrigue hastened U.S. annexation of Texas in 1845 by a bare majority of Congress, supported by a slave-owning Administration, both fearing British motives as they welcomed a new slave-state into the Union.

Another challenge laid at capitalism's door arises from the Parliamentary payment of £20 million to the unpopular West Indian slave-holders for the emancipation of their 780,000 slaves. Such an unprecedented payment for an evil, in an amount equal to forty per cent of the government's total revenue in 1833, could hardly rest well with the abolitionists, let alone the working-class. Viewed in the context of an oligarchical government venerating property, three decades before our Civil War, the price was deemed worth the vote, especially since the conservative House of Lords could veto the legislation. Additionally, the patrolling of the seas against the slave trade, and the sponsorship of indentured emigrants and ex-slaves in the West Indies, drove the costs up substantially. In capitalism's defense, the decision of Pitt and his colleagues to put so much government money on the line with their newly-found sensibilities was a redemptive act.

It was not Drescher's mission to redeem capitalism in his *Capitalism and Antislavery* (1987), although he uses Eric Williams' work as a point of departure. His important contribution was to document beyond question the extraordinary use of a popular mandate to enforce a political decision, the gathering of hundreds of thousands of signatures on antislavery petitions to Parliament over the period 1788–1833. The mass petition campaign, supported by newspaper advertisements and a sugar boycott, was a watershed in the development of effective public opinion. Starting in Manchester, a hard-nosed manufacturing city, with much to lose from the end of slave-cotton, if that should occur as a domino-effect in America, the flood of petitions impelled England to cross the 'psychological threshold' into the abolition era, beyond the hopes of the originating Quaker religionists, who envisaged a long period of reforms at best.[29]

Further Drescher has analyzed the occupations of the petition-signers in order to counterbalance or moderate the emphasis of his colleagues like Roger Anstey and David Brion Davis, who argue that Christian evangelicalism, in league with the so-called 'Saints', men like Clarkson, Sharp and Wilberforce, was the primary force of English abolitionist history. Acknowledging the role of religion in his search, Drescher finds the Methodists to be the paradigm antislavery religious group. In that group, his analysis identifies as most significant an 'artisan' class – not the expected middle class – among the signers. The artisans ranked above the masses of wage-earners. They were small employers in manufacturing, mining and commerce cast up by the industrial revolution in the thousands to meet the needs of the infant capitalist factories and mills. Presumably these artisans were fiercely independent, as averse to forced labor on plantations as they would be to becoming factory hands themselves. The Drescher hypothesis finds their presence in America as well, and concludes there was an essential fusion of artisans, non-slave owning capitalists and intellectuals on a world-wide scale behind the successful anti-slavery movements.[30] On this basis, I have 'drafted' Drescher to testify to capitalism's redemption in the matter of slavery, aware that such hypotheses overlap and compete in the rich historiography of the subject.[31]

* * *

For those interested in intellectual history, David Brion Davis is unrivalled in his treatment of slavery. He constructs a broad fabric that goes to the heart of the human condition, a mix of history, economics, psychology, religion and moral considerations that help us see ourselves and our limitations through the institution. Grounded in scholarly research on the subject, he does not hesitate to explore relationships and proposals that transcend concrete history and traditional disciplines.

From this view, Davis' *Slávery and Human Progress* (1984), a study in preparation for his third and final volume on 'the problems of slavery', affords an insight into the role of capitalism. That slavery is a problematic rather than a clear-cut aberration is demonstrated by Davis as he reveals its moral ambiguities, such as the hope for emancipation combined with the whip, the symbiotic relationship between master and slave, and the constant claims for public sanction.

In the same sense in which we have depicted capitalism's role in creating and ending slavery, Davis develops a powerful analogue of slavery and material and spiritual progress over the centuries. He is particularly eloquent on the relations between slavery and human progress conceived as a linear, open-ended, optimistic vision of steady reform and improvement. This modern version departs radically from belief in progress as a recurring cycle of golden ages, as conceived in classical thought. It also departs from the European age of faith that conceptualized the road to progress as a heavenly destination. Though slavery long preceded and survived these visions, its greatest anomaly derives from having flourished in the era of progressive optimism, distinguished by Newtonian science and Enlightenment reason. It was an era that claimed 600,000 Civil War dead and left America with its bleeding racial crisis.

Against this background, Davis confirms the role of capitalism, with its technology and insatiable profit motive, as the agent of material progress enabling the revitalized Europeans to enslave millions of blacks while conquering a good part of the world in a short span of history. Where then were the restraining limitations on capitalism? Where were the institutions of power and tradition that might have closed the moral borders crossed by the upstart economic system?

In my opinion, three moral guardians can be held accountable. First, organized religion; second, the values of the society that sanctioned modern slavery at its peak; and finally, errant capitalism, mending its ways and gaining absolution with its logic of free markets and free labor. The three components overlap, of course, and each finds supporters and detractors from the safe haven of the present. The important matter is they were sufficiently in congruence to effect a political end to slavery as a worldwide economic institution in the nineteenth century.

Judaism, Christianity and Islam from their inceptions had a durable accommodation with slavery. The Hebrew Bible, with its Exodus and its concept of the Jubilee, during which slaves were freed, reverberates through the centuries. Christianity, the major religion of western civilization, the religion of choice for slaves and the humble of the Roman Empire, played the most paradoxical role. It took nineteen centuries to reject slavery, compared with market capitalism's rejection while capitalism was still in its swaddling clothes.

This assertion requires refuting claims that capitalism succeeded on Southern plantations, and might have continued to do so for generations, if left alone. An alternate answer is that Southern plantation agriculture was more feudal and siegneurial than modern capitalism could tolerate. This choice gains credibility because it is advanced with careful support by Eugene D. Genovese, a highly respected figure in American slavery history.[32] At any rate, the linkage was doomed if the ethos or spirit of capitalism, rather than the bottom line of its plantation accounting, is admitted as evidence. Recall Max Weber's *The Protestant Ethic and the Spirit of Capitalism* (1904–5). Weber stipulates he would not be willing to claim the 'ethic' alone produced capitalism. He simply found the ethic and the spirit mutually reinforcing at a certain stage and place in history. By analogy, the spirit of capitalism, especially in relation to its Calvinist work ethic, was dysfunctional with Protestant Anglo-American plantation society in the nineteenth century. Adam Smith recognized this contradiction for his own century, but faces the claim of other guardians that he predicted a long road to abolition, thereby diminishing the effect of capitalism's contribution. Again the time factor is relative. The fact remains that the founder of capitalist theory, a friend and confidante of business leaders, recognized the inevitability of abolition, and held slaveholders in contempt.[33]

If the spirit of Christianity was weak when antislavery sentiments appeared, what antidote regenerated it? The English clergy had an existential advantage over their colleagues in the American South, since English slavery was overseas and not an organic part of their society's daily life and bread. Still, as the Quakers expressed doubts in their Philadelphia Meeting of 1758, and then disowned slave dealers from their ranks in 1761, practically all Christian clergy on both continents, including the American North, closed ranks on slavery's side. The preferred strategy in the early days of abolition was to draw heavily on the Bible for justification, certainly not to rely on the conversion mission that animated the Catholic Iberians. Nor could the clergy rely with enthusiasm on classical, and therefore pagan, philosophy's comfort with slavery. Their own Enlightenment philosophers, men like Adam Smith, John Millar, Benjamin Franklin, Thomas Jefferson, and later, John Stuart Mill and Ralph Waldo Emerson, were troublesome enough, grounding their moral antipathy to slavery basically on economic grounds, that it impeded progress, downgrading religion on either side of the argument.[34] Speaking from the authority of their pulpits to church-going majorities, the clergy cited fundamental Scripture: Leviticus 25, authorizing Jews to buy 'the children of strangers... as your bondsmen forever.' Additionally the New Testament did not prohibit slavery. Indeed the use of 'bondservant' in the speech of Jesus, and the metaphor of 'slaves of Christ' by Saint Paul, could be interpreted as implicit recognition of the institution.

Religion in the period of abolition was a clamorous, public matter, involving doctrine and class, amply recorded elsewhere. In summary, Davis asserts the great divide in relation to slavery in England was the recognition by both clergy and the devout abolitionist leaders that traditional Christianity, with its promise of long-range salvation and heavenly freedom, was inadequate for the day. It was necessary to translate the millennial, eschatological promise, which had encouraged passivity, into an immediate demand for victory over a self-evident evil. Only then could the powers of slavery be banished and Christianity become an agent of spiritual progress in a material world. Not the least of this inspiration derived from the opportunity to strike back at the *philosophes* and rationalists of the Enlightenment, scoffers like Voltaire and Hume who had announced Christianity's fall and its irrelevance to freedom. Even excessively liberal Christians, the perpetrators of the '*trahison des clercs*' through their modernity, science and philosophy, would be rebuffed.[35] Whatever the formula, Christian leadership against slavery was decisive. Slavery was abolished in 1833, twenty-six years after the closing of the slave trade, and a precedent was set for America. Christianity had fallen and redeemed itself. Granted the metaphor of redemption is far more suitable for Christianity than for capitalism, the latter still demonstrated its moral potential.

* * *

Can we briefly summarize with any accuracy the values of an age? Probably not, but changes in sensibilities may help. In England, abolition occurred four years before Victoria's ascension, initiating a long period of publicly sanctioned morality and imperial capitalist arrogance, including dominion over millions of dark-skinned subjects. Still a case can be made that there was a softening of sensibilities in the mother country. There was an increase in altruism, philanthropy, aesthetic and intellectual concerns, prison reform, asylums and a host of voluntary agencies like the Salvation Army, all greatly fuelled by the bourgeois religious values of the new capitalist class, empowered by tremendous wealth and seeking social approval.[36] Slavery was an open target in such a century.

Europeans saw America as a vast land of potential industrial rivalry, westward expansion and peoples' presidents like Jackson and Lincoln. In England, the raw demands on human labor and natural resources imposed by the unregulated technology would be harshly described by writers like Dickens, Carlyle and the astute Tocqueville. In America, Mark Twain was a typical literary favorite. His Huck Finn, on a raft on the Mississippi with his fugitive-slave friend Jim, speculated, as his country did, on the double-bind of morality that told him slavery was wrong, but if society sanctioned it, it must be right.[37] Clearly America was not a clone of England in its slavery problem, ready to topple the institution once the mother country showed the way. The North and South were different countries, far less reconcilable than Disraeli's 'two nations' of rich and poor in England.[38]

* * *

One more moral guardian should be held accountable, the law and its judiciary. In 1772, Chief Justice Mansfield, in the Somerset case, ruled that no support for slavery in England could be found in the common law, though he managed to exclude the colonies from his ruling. The case arose from fugitives or slaves brought to England by their masters, the slaves thereby claiming freedom. The reluctant Chief Justice, while supporting the slaves, made it clear that he was still interested in preserving property rights of masters in the colonies, where such rights mattered. Though the case therefore had narrow application, it symbolized the contradiction of slavery with English political freedom, and the general distaste for supporting a master's excessive claims. It was also a rejection of the elaborate Justinian Code of absolute ownership of slaves bequeathed by the Roman jurists, a model employed by other slaveholding nations for centuries.[39] In that respect, it was an institutional inspiration for eventual abolition by Parliamentary statute in 1833.

A consequence on the positive side from the English precedent can be found in the dilemma faced by the Southern judges in antebellum America. Mark Tushnet, in *The American Law of Slavery, 1810–1860* (1957), contends that moral sensibilities, or considerations of humanity, posed a dilemma for judges ordinarily disposed to rule in favor of the economic or property interests of slaveholders. Examining at length representative appellate cases in three Southern states, he concludes the eminent judges wrestled with but could not accommodate the conflicting claims.[40]

On balance, the decisions rejected slaveholders' claims for relief from harsh or negligent treatment. Although Tushnet categorizes the slaveholders' interests as 'capitalist property interests' in contention with non-capitalist moral sensibilities, an alternate conclusion may be drawn. There is no *a priori* basis for assuming either that plantation slavery was typical of modern capitalism, or that the judges, trained in common law, did not share in the bourgeois values we have noted.

72

Certainly their moral concern about the limits of property rights compares favorably with the monstrous error of Supreme Court Justice Taney and his colleagues in 1857 that Dred Scott, claiming freedom on grounds similar to those of the Somerset case, had no standing in the court since he was black.

* * *

What conclusions can we draw from our analogue of slavery? One, favor a healthy ingestion of skepticism when presented with claims of moral sanction or superiority. Another, withhold full faith in institutions, however authoritative or long-lasting. Conversely, give benefit to the capacities of institutions to change, even to redeem themselves. Still another, beware of hegemonies of power, such as the complex of sanctimony, the profit motive and nationalism that supported slavery. As for history, neither material determinism nor great men theories carry the day: social institutions, economic forces and abolitionist heroes together ended slavery. Similarly, we should question imposing claims, such as slavery was 'indispensable' for developing the New World, or the United States was 'defined' by a Civil War that might have been avoided. All other modern slave nations elected compensation or gradual transition. Finally, we should concede that capitalism ended on the positive side of the slavery problem by the skin of its teeth. Can it rely on a providential relationship such as 'free market-free labor' in future crises? Or should it seek moral limitations, such as 'social justice' criteria? A final analogue, the case of American constitutional law as institutional success in limiting capitalism, will be developed in Chapters 5 and 6, leading to additional moral theory considerations and some proposed agenda in the concluding Chapters 7 and 8.

Notes

1 For ancient slavery, see Finley, *Ancient Slavery & Modern Ideology*, 19–26. Finley supports economic preference as basic cause, but notes that nineteenth-century historians generally missed the point, either

dismissing ancient slavery as a peripheral aberration, or treating it as a moral problem. (The persistence of slavery as highly-charged metaphor is illustrated by the attacks on Hillary Clinton, in the 1992 Presidential campaign, for comparing marriage with slavery. In context, her analysis was historically correct and non-controversial. That is, from ancient times through the mid-nineteenth century, married women were legally subordinated to their husbands.)

2 Capitalist prototypes are rarely mentioned in slavery history, which generally has an anti-capitalist bias. A strong example would be James Cropper, a devout Quaker, wealthy Liverpool merchant, and disciple of Adam Smith. He merged his religious zeal with Adam Smith's concept of self-interest for entrepreneurs, to whom he added slaveholders, as the formula for abolition. Cropper became a major figure, publicist and fund-raiser for the movement in both England and America. See David Brion Davis, *Slavery and Human Progress* (New York: Oxford University Press, 1984), 179–81.

3 Adam Smith, *An Inquiry into the Nature and Causes of the Wealth of Nations* ed. Edwin Cannan (New York, 1937, orig. 1776), 80.

4 Davis, *Slavery and Human Progress*, 107–230.

5 Seymour Drescher, *Capitalism and Antislavery: British Mobilization in Comparative Perspective* (New York: Oxford University Press, 1987), 135–66. See also Drescher, *Econocide: British Slavery in the Era of Abolition* (Pittsburgh: University of Pittsburgh Press, 1977). In both books, Drescher minimizes the role of capitalism in effecting abolition.

6 Geoffrey Barraclough, ed., *The Times Atlas of World History* (Maplewood: Hammond Inc., 1979), 120.

7 Lynn Whyte, Jr., *Medieval Technology and Social Change* (Oxford: Oxford University Press, 1962), 1979 edition, 56.

8 Frederic C. Lane, *Venice: A Maritime Republic* (Baltimore: Johns Hopkins University Press, 1973), 151–68.

9 Davis, *Slavery and Human Progress*, 54–5.

10 Robert William Fogel and Stanley L. Engerman, *Time on the Cross: The Economics of American Negro Slavery* (Boston: Little, Brown), 1974, vol. I, 67–86. For rebuttal, and counter-rebuttal, see *American Economic Review* 69 (1979) and 70 (1982). Orlando Patterson, *Slavery and Social Death*, 33, asserts the South's plantations were 'thoroughly capitalistic',

adding to Fogel and Engerman's argument that all slaves were 'totally flexible', that is, they could be 'perfect capitalist slaves' as well as non-capitalist retainer, concubine, or soldier slaves. (For *contra*, see ahead in this chapter.) See also Robert William Fogel, *Without Consent or Contract: The Rise and Fall of American Slavery* (New York: W.W. Norton, 1990). This book repeats the capitalist hypothesis, but adds a broad treatment of social, religious and political developments. It also disowns any moral approval or justification for the economic success on the plantations, capitalist or otherwise. On receipt of the Nobel Prize in Economics for 1993, Fogel reiterated his disclaimer: 'That was the lesson. Morality is a higher human goal than just efficiency.' *Los Angeles Times*, 12 October 1993, D4.

11 P. A. Brunt, *Italian Manpower 225 BC – AD 14* (New York: Oxford University Press, 1971), 367–88.

12 Finley, *Ancient Slavery & Modern Ideology*, 123–49.

13 Patterson, *Slavery and Social Death*, 17–77. Patterson defines slavery as a special form of human parasitism, or dependency, involving the use of authority (power, punishment, fear, etc.), alienation (denatalization, no roots, no marriage, etc.), and social death (dishonor, segregation, etc.).

14 David Henige, *In Search of Columbus: The Sources of the First Voyage*, (Tucson: University of Arizona Press, 1991). Las Casas' book was discovered in a private library in 1790.

15 Judith N. Shklar, *Ordinary Vices* (Cambridge: Harvard University Press, 1984), 7–44.

16 Qu. in J. H. Elliott, 'The World After Columbus', *New York Review of Books*, 10 October 1991, 14.

17 Davis, *Slavery and Human Progress*, 74.

18 Roughly another 250,000 Portuguese emigrated to Asian possessions in the sixteenth century. But Europeans were unable to establish more than coastal enclaves at that time, contending with peoples whose military and commercial skills matched or excelled their own. Elliott, 'The World After Columbus', 10.

19 Sherburne F. Cook and Woodrow Borah, *Essays in Population History: Mexico and the Caribbean* (Berkeley, 1977), qu. in Davis, *Slavery and Human Progress*, 64–5. Patterson, *Slavery and Social Death*, 113, qu. Kenneth Andrews, *The Spanish Caribbean: Trade and Plunder*

1530–1630 (New Haven: Yale University Press, 1978), reports only 1 million Arawaks extinguished in Hispaniola in the same period, compared with Cook and Borah's 7–8 million. Slave statistics generally do not show such a discrepancy.

20 Davis, *Slavery and Human Progress*, 70.

21 James S. Fishkin, *The Limits of Obligation* (New Haven: Yale University Press, 1982), 20–4.

22 Davis, *Slavery and Human Progress*, 71.

23 The accepted sources for these figures are the pioneering estimates of Philip D. Curtin, revised by Paul E. Lovejoy, 'The Volume of the Atlantic Slave Trade: A Synthesis', *Journal of African History*, 23 (1982) 473–501.

24 Ken Burns, producer of the documentary 'The Civil War', quotes from a letter received from a slave descendant: '…such dignity in the archival faces of my people, who were enslaved but who never surrendered their souls to slavery.' *Los Angeles Times*, 8 May 1992, B9.

25 Patterson, *Slavery and Social Death*, 115–19, 397, n.54. Also see Katia M. de Queirōs Mattoso, *To Be a Slave in Brazil 1550–1888* (New Brunswick: Rutgers University Press, 1986), 15–25. In this connection, I discussed the complicity of Africans in delivering slaves with David L. Wolper on 12 December 1991. Wolper's TV miniseries production of 'Roots' in 1977 was viewed by 130 million people, then the largest TV audience in history. 'Roots' was a force in raising consciousness in America about black slavery, as well as black pride, beyond measure. Wolper states he and author Alex Haley were aware of the problem but did not emphasize it, having enough at stake in getting the program aired in the first place.

26 Patterson, *Slavery and Social Death*, 162.

27 Eric Williams, *Capitalism and Slavery* (Chapel Hill: University of North Carolina Press, 1944).

28 Drescher, *Capitalism and Antislavery*, 7–10.

29 *Ibid.*, 71.

30 *Ibid.*, 134.

31 For Drescher's refutation of Williams' charge that the abolition movement was a capitalist distraction to head off working-class dissatisfaction, see

Capitalism and Antislavery, chapters 7 and 8. In effect, the working-class supported abolition, and the period was one of general harmony and interest in reform in England.

32 Eugene D. Genovese, *Roll, Jordan, Roll: The World the Slaves Made* (New York: Pantheon Books, 1974).

33 Adam Smith, *Lectures on Jurisprudence*, R.L. Meek *et al.*, eds., (Oxford, 1978), 186–7, 206.

34 Adam Smith's close friend, David Hume, is excluded from this list because of his specious reasoning on racial inferiority; John Locke, because although he wrote eloquently about 'vile Slavery', he still managed to hold shares in the Royal African Company and to provide for slavery in the constitution he proposed for the colony of Carolina. Jefferson just manages inclusion; although a slaveholder, he was against slavery. Gore Vidal, a novelist with a firm grasp on American history, cannot forgive Jefferson, who he claims would not free his slaves because they constituted the bulk of his estate.

35 Davis, *Slavery and Human Progress*, 119–22. Even so major a figure as David Brion Davis faces pitfalls in the competitive, highly-charged field of slavery history. After writing an apparently laudatory review of Thomas Slaughter's *Bloody Dawn: The Christiana Riot and Racial Violence in the Antebellum North* (New York: Oxford University Press, 1991) in *The New York Review of Books*, 30 January 1992, he was on the receiving line for Slaughter's letter to the Editor in the 23 April 1992 issue. Slaughter denounced Davis' 'greater role for Protestant ministers in the history of racial violence than for the working-class whites and blacks who actually shed blood. Such, though, is the prejudice of Davis and so many historians of his generation. They would rather study the texts of dead, white liberal men than comb the archives for evidence about the lives of poor and working-class folks about whom they have little knowledge and less understanding.' For Davis' reply, see the same issue. Also, see Davis' 'Terror in Mississippi', *New York Review of Books*, 4 November 1993, in which Davis lauds extensive new research in slavery records that prove conclusively a significant readiness on the part of slaves to rebel violently against their masters in the early period of the Civil War. This contradicts much of conventional slavery history.

36 See Thomas Haskell, 'Capitalism and the Origins of the Humanitarian Sensibility: Some Analytical Considerations', *American Historical Review* 90:2 (April and June, 1985). See Davis, *Slavery and Human*

Progress, 351, n.7. See also Thomas Bender, ed., *The Antislavery Debate* (Berkeley: University of California Press, 1992), in which the Haskell thesis is debated as a problem in historical interpretation by John Ashworth, David Brion Davis and Thomas Haskell. While Davis still maintains capitalists were more beneficiaries than conscious agents of antislavery, he concludes: 'Still I am convinced now, as in 1975, that the growth and triumphs of antislavery had the long-term effect, regardless of the abolitionist intentions, of legitimating and morally sustaining the new industrial capitalist order.' 308–9.

37 Mark Twain, *The Adventures of Huckleberry Finn*, (orig. 1884; New York: Bantam, 1981), 85.

38 For the persistence of inequality in America, emphasizing race, see Andrew Hacker, *Two Nations: Black and White, Separate, Hostile, Unequal* (New York: Scribner's, 1992). Hacker questions the 'extra patience and perseverance we ask of blacks' that we have never required of ourselves, a warning later confirmed in the May 1992 tragedy in Los Angeles. He concludes: 'Race has made America its prisoner since the first chattels were landed on these shores...' He does not hold the present condition as accountable to capitalism, since racial attitudes cut across all levels of the 'white nation'. See also Nicholas Lemann, *The Promised Land: The Great Black Migration and How It Changed America* (New York: Alfred A. Knopf, 1991). Lemann traces the dislocations and urban problems arising from the mass migration to the northern cities in the World War II era and states: '...to be born into a [black] ghetto is to be consigned to a fate that no American should have to suffer.'

39 Both Patterson and Davis stress the fine point that common law differs from Roman law because common law, in relation to property, is based on the relations of power one person holds over another, not on absolute ownership. See Patterson, *Slavery and Social Death*, 27–32, and Davis, *Slavery and Human Progress*, 323, n.14. Seymour Drescher has rightly called my attention to the importance of the English common law tradition that sustained a libertarian sentiment well before modern slavery arose and served to insulate the mother country from its establishment at home. Similar legal and philosophic traditions prevailed in other Northwestern European countries, relegating slavery to overseas possessions. In that sense, the 'sea-change' in thought that abolished slavery was the result of a gathering storm, and even John Locke's public detestation of the institution is less questionable.

40 Mark Tushnet, *The American Law of Slavery, 1810–1860: Considerations of Humanity and Interest* (Princeton: Princeton University Press, 1981). I do not wish to downgrade Tushnet's exemplary work by using it to enhance my capitalist bias. There is a highly valuable school of slavery history in the Marxist tradition, under the leadership of Eugene D. Genovese and Elizabeth Fox-Genovese, that often sees through the masks of illusion, distortion, and social convention that blur the vision of less-disciplined and critical observers. There is a high interest in slavery among Marxists, probably because of their ability to see social injustice in terms of the 'social relations of production' and the motivations of the class presumably controlling these relations. They also identify capitalism as an exercise of power over others in ways not easily evident to capitalists, who feel constantly challenged by the state, the media, church, intellectuals and labor. Marx apparently was not particularly interested in slavery, aside from its place in the stages of economic history, as well as a sober analysis of its attraction where land was not scarce and therefore labor was hard to assemble in groups, the last item being of equal interest to Adam Smith. Conceivably Marx backed away from indicting capitalism as responsible for continuing slavery because he was quite appreciative of capitalism's free labor component. Marx as enthusiast in that respect is evidenced by his admiration for Lincoln, the capitalist Emancipator, in the Vienna *Presse* of October 12, 1862: '...the Proclamation [is] the most important document of American history since the founding of the Union... In the history of the United States and in the history of humanity, Lincoln occupies a place beside Washington!' (qu. in Davis, *Slavery and Human Progress*, 248.) For a balanced view, see Steven Lukes, *Marxism and Morality* (Oxford: Clarendon Press, 1985). Lukes finds little of importance in relation to slavery, but sees a distinct advantage in marxist (lowercase 'M' preferred by Lukes) methodology, excised of its crude ends-means fallacy, for determining a moral approach to economic problems.

5 The Court and capitalism: an analogue of institutional success

1 *Smith* v. *Tax Court* (1999)

Nine justices in black robes file out, another day's work done, on April 2, 1999.

The case has been brought by Smith, who challenges the Internal Revenue Service for demanding special taxes unconstitutionally, he believes, since the taxes involve the radical Guaranteed Work Act, passed by Congress in 1997. The Court accepts the case. Another tax crank, say the watchers, but the Court feels the constitutionality of the Act should be faced.

On June 1, 1999, the Court sustains the legislation by a 5 to 4 majority, subject to reservations. Since the Chief Justice is in the majority, she designates herself to write the opinion. It is non-traditional, part narrative, part economic, often subjective. The Chief Justice wants to explain and justify, the issue being momentous.

First, the narrative. The Act, not to be confused with 'right to work' nomenclature preempted by union opponents, guarantees employment for all Americans able and willing to work. Passed by a bipartisan majority in both House and Senate, and influenced by a groundswell of grass-roots pressure, the Act is signed by a President threatened with an amendment should he exercise his veto. The Act has been the law of the land for two years.

It specifies that all men and women, age 18 to 62, not otherwise exempted but able to work, must pay a substantial tax to forego the new benefit, in order to help defray the expense of bringing marginal workers into the labor force. Known as the 'sloth tax', reminiscent of the 'sin taxes' of previous decades, its even-handedness has gained public support. It demonstrates the Act is non-coercive – you don't have to work – and it satisfies workers in the knowledge that they can create their own sabbaticals, should the occasion arise. Over a half-million sloths voluntarily pay $100 monthly, subject to cost-of-living increases, for the privilege of not working, using savings, inheritances and underground income to pay their taxes, netting a half-billion dollars annually for the budget process. Not surprisingly, considering their contribution, they are regarded as admirable non-conformists, located in the creative, high-spending consumer segment of the nation's demography, and not in the unemployed segment. When they return to work, carrying their portable pensions and national health insurance (but debited for Social Security increments), they are welcomed by private industry with above-average jobs, the employers discerning commitment in the preference for work. Moreover, the government, appropriately tough-minded about these idealists, collects over 90% of sloth taxes due, through alliances with state auto-licensing bureaus.

A second feature of this legislation, the Chief Justice noted, was the creation of a permanent public works program as employer of last resort, eliminating the fear that labor would be forced on private employers, already burdened with training and education for the disabled and disadvantaged under equal opportunity laws. About 800,000 guaranteed workers, mostly young and from ethnic minorities, all voluntary recruits, are sheltered in former military bases and similar installations. They are engaged, at below-market wages, in helping to restore and maintain the country's infrastructure, including roads, bridges, dams, harbors, waste facilities, fire and flood control, and natural resources.

Older claimants are offered employment, combining below-market paychecks with job-training, in nearby school systems, health services and other public agencies, or on public construction projects, mainly in the inner cities. More qualified applicants are absorbed as super-numeraries in the long-term government infrastructure program contracted to private employers and concentrating on high-speed transportation, communications and product research laboratories. All concerned admit the guaranteed work force is inefficient and subsidized, but it is work and not dole. The Secretary of Industrial Policy (formerly Commerce) has endorsed the Act as a contribution to the nation's competitive economic strategy. The Secretary of Health and Human Services has demonstrated a connection between sharply reduced crime and drug statistics and the employment, health-indoctrination and skill-training offered young people who had given up on work. Labor leaders, in return for the long-sought goal, reluctantly accept the sabotage of market wages, so long as they exceed minimum wages. Employers applaud the major cost reductions in their unemployment and workers compensation insurance. Economists are optimistic about the exponential effects of the cash flow on investment and eventual tax receipts, and the Budget Office sees gains whenever direct paychecks are substituted for inefficient, high-overhead 'welfare net' expenditures. The moral and psychological benefits of work, the Chief Justice conceded, are not the business of the Court.

In fact, she noted, the Chief Justice should not be seen as a cheerleader for a government experiment whose life is at stake in the case before the Court (other than resurrection by amendment under Article V), and certainly not when four of her colleagues consider the Act an unconstitutional exercise of power by Congress.

* * *

Yet judges must consider reality, she continued, as well as dominant public opinion. Nor should they exclude themselves from sociological and economic information, now so fully available. As the bimillenial approaches, the preoccupying subject in America is work for those wanting to work. The fear of unemployment, as well as the dismal figures themselves, had persisted for a decade, in spite of traditional government spending, taxing and monetary strategies, and a bipartisan commitment to economic growth. The majority agreed, she stated, with a theory of unemployment stasis sufficient to justify the Act as purposeful and rational, despite the magnitude of its reach as a peacetime measure. Briefly, previous stages of economic growth, absorbing waves of immigration, were based on open land, undeveloped natural resources, technological innovation, especially in transportation and

82

communications, primacy in heavy industry, world trade dominion, and wars or the preparation for wars. Most of these had disappeared or matured, and present technology tended to reduce jobs through gains in labor productivity, as it had for agricultural production. The people, unlike their predecessors in the Great Depression, appear unwilling to wait for the economic system to wring itself out through recurrent cycles. Those at the bottom claim civil rights a hollow victory without the right to work. If work is a fundamental right, as the Act implies, government logically must be employer of last resort. Otherwise the Act would be only symbolic, like President Truman's Employment Act of 1946.

Purposeful and rational, but constitutional? Yes, first on the doctrine that Congress has implied powers, in addition to the powers expressly granted in the document. It mattered little that Chief Justice Marshall hammered out the doctrine in *McCullough* v. *Maryland* (1819), presiding in the remote Court quarters under the Senate Chamber, and in a case motivated by partisan politics over the continued existence of the Bank of the United States, which Marshall sustained against Maryland's objections. Marshall's vision of a strong national government, superior to state or regional interests, required that broad economic powers be vested in Congress. The doctrine had served the country well, she stated, opening the way to eliminating tariffs and roadblocks among the states, securing the credit and legitimacy of the federal government, and fathering a group of useful economic regulatory agencies such as the Interstate Commerce Commission (1887) and Federal Trade Commission (1914). Further support for the doctrine could be found in Article I, Section 8, [18], requiring that such laws be 'necessary and proper', easily exploited on the side of Congress. Additionally, the Preamble to the Constitution, stating the purpose 'to promote the general welfare', and its repetition in Article I, Section 8, [1], expanded Congressional capacity to enact unenumerated social objectives, such as the Guaranteed Work Act. On these foundations, the peacetime precedent of Roosevelt's Works Progress Administration, employing at its peak 3.5 millions, had been established.

On a secondary scale, the Chief Justice asserted, validation can be drawn from the Fifth Amendment provision that no person can be deprived of life, liberty, or property without due process. Applying the examples of restrictions on liberty now denied to the states through the Fourteenth Amendment, the majority interpreted denial of work as deprivation of a fundamental condition without which liberty is an illusion. Similarly the Court's expansion over the years of the Commerce Clause (Article I, Section 8, [3]) justified its extension to the Act. It reasoned so on the grounds of disruption of commerce inherent in chronic unemployment at a high level, analogous to the constitutional precedent that found labor legislation an antidote to disruptive strikes inhibiting commerce.[1] Finally, in a philosophic vein, the Chief Justice admitted she had wrestled deeply with the underlying basic question, did the anti-market Act, mandating work on demand, threaten the existence of capitalism, the traditional, consensually-approved economic system? Aside from the changing forms of capitalism itself, both in America and abroad, she found guidance in Justice Holmes' dissent in *Lochner* v. *New York* (1905):

> [A] constitution is not intended to embody a particular economic theory, whether of paternalism and the organic relation of the citizen to the State or of laissez-faire. It is made for people of fundamentally differing views, and the accident of our finding certain opinions natural and familiar, or novel and even shocking, ought not to conclude our judgment upon the question whether statutes embodying them conflict with the Constitution of the United States.[2]

* * *

The Chief Justice concluded with the Court's reservations. Although it had voted to sustain the Act by a 5 to 4 vote, the Court unanimously rejected the section known as the 'sloth tax'. Though the government advocates had listed a wide array of existing tax variations from neutrality – anti-progressive sales taxes, differing estate and income tax rates in the states, deductions and privileges in the Internal Revenue Code – the Court as one ruled the sloth-tax constituted an invidious distinction and was punitive in the bargain. Noting the Court's historical preference not to interfere with tax legislation, a single case was cited. *Harper* v. *Board of Elections* (1966) concerned a Virginia statute requiring a modest poll tax as a condition for voting eligibility. The Court had ruled against Virginia on grounds of

84

interference with a fundamental right, Justice Black supplying the lone dissent. In summary, the Court ordered Congress to phase out the tax with due diligence and to provide compensation in cash or tax credits for Smith and his fellow sloths.

* * *

The dissenting opinion came from one of the Court's most brilliant members: 'Sheer nonsense! Not only the sloth-tax but the entire Act should have been overruled. This is interpretation of implied powers and fundamental rights with a rubber band. At the very least, the Act should have gone back to Congress for the amendment process, where the cold water of time might expose its folly. Will America never learn? The whole world is rushing to the free market and we put the deadweight of drones on the public payroll without duration or qualification. The stasis theory is smoke.

Look at Germany, Japan, the Four Little Dragons! How many more impediments can our system take before crashing in ruins like Diocletian amidst his price edicts? Schumpeter was right: the social engineers have mesmerized the politicians. Together they are nailing the coffin of capitalism.'

2 The Court in the Marshall Period

As the hypothetical case suggests, even a Guaranteed Work Act, antipathetic to efficient capitalism but sponsored by a frustrated people and their majoritarian Congress, would not founder in the Court. In other capitalist countries, notably England, France, and Italy, without a Court as arbiter of legislation, successive cabinet governments have nationalized and denationalized basic industries with even less suspense and fanfare. Capitalism is not an establishment religion. Probably the only instance of its designation by provision is in the Republic of China-British Joint Declaration of 1984, which stipulates that Hong Kong can maintain its capitalist system for at least fifty years after the takeover takes effect in 1997.

The Constitution does create a special place for property – the private property essential to capitalism – in the 'life, liberty and property' phrasing of the Fifth Amendment, which we noted in Chapter 1 supplanted Jefferson's less-worldly 'happiness' objective. The Founders were men of property, their Revolution had been over economic as well as political grievances, and their respect for property as a stabilizing influence and goal for human endeavor helped shape the Constitution.[3] A case can be made that the elevation of property as a restraint on democracy permitted the bold experiment in popular sovereignty, and providentially stimulated as a by-product the country's tremendous economic growth.

This growth had a threefold effect. It enabled America to open its doors to tens of millions of emigrants needed for the workforce, including the immediate ancestors of most of the readers of this book. It enabled America to become a world power and model for democratic government. Finally, it enabled the capitalist system to redeem and reform itself, as the price to be paid for its dominance.

It would be distortion to deny the reality of nineteenth and early twentieth-century capitalism, an arena of harshly repressive labor policies, unacceptable working and living conditions, and epic financial chicanery. The efforts of distinguished economists, such as F.A. Hayek, cannot adequately revise this record, but their injunction to see history in terms of context and possibilities is valid.[4] So, perhaps, is the reminder that the 'workshop of democracy', (James MacGregor Burns' phrase), was a capitalist workshop. The property-oriented system, legitimated by the Supreme Court, flourished – with certain exceptions – until the Great Depression era. Then the Court, by necessity, it seemed, downgraded the priority of property, although not sufficiently, some say. Such considerations, related to alternative constitutional theories of intent, rights, interpretation, and procedure, are a matter of constant debate.

For the present, we can demonstrate that the Court's historic effect on capitalism has been an institutional success, one that has expanded capitalism's moral as well as practical claims. To do this, a review of landmark economic cases, uncomplicated by partisan theory, will serve us best. For those like myself, who advocate regulated, constantly-reforming capitalism, the examples are admittedly rare in the long period of laissez-faire capitalism that existed from the founding until the New Deal era. Still, we are grounded in our past, and understanding the Court and capitalism starts with Chief Justice Marshall, a Revolutionary War army officer at Valley Forge in his twenties, self-trained lawyer and successful politician, considering the political and economic destiny of thirteen fractious states made one by the Constitution.

Marshall's accomplishments in constitutional interpretation during the Court's early period are well-known. Chief Justice for 34 years (1801–1835), he led the Court in establishing implied powers for Congress in the above *McCullough* v. *Maryland* case, and judicial review of all legislative acts, federal and state, in *Marbury* v. *Madison* (1803), infuriating President Jefferson in the latter case.[5] These were key doctrines in the Court's assumption of its role in the infant Republic, and have no moral or fairness relevance. Yet Marshall's vision of a strong, federally supreme government, able to expand nationally and overcome intense regional differences of interest, had a moral consequence. Only such a Union could withstand the Founders' avoidance of the slavery issue in their Constitution, other than incorporating it as a property concept, authorizing the return of fugitive slaves to slave-state owners, as it did in Article 4, Section 2, [3], counting each slave as three-fifths of a person for Congressional apportionment purposes (Article I, Section 1, [3]), and establishing the proviso to end the slave-trade, as noted in Chapter 4. Without judicial supremacy and review, the government faced nullification of antislavery legislation for new states and territories by the five slave-states, including Marshall's own Virginia. Capitalism's redemptive role in regard to slavery, a moral as well as economic aberration, has been analyzed in the previous chapter.[6]

3 The Court in the Laissez-Faire Period

The Steamboat Monopoly Cases

The Court as reformer of dominant capitalism in the laissez-faire period made an initial appearance in the Steamboat Monopoly cases. Monopoly and price-fixing, as Adam Smith warned, were the enemies of 'natural liberty', Smith's general term for his still-unnamed capitalist system. These impediments belonged to the rival school of state-sponsored mercantilism, which he urged his fellow Englishmen to foreswear in order to gain the rewards of the market system. The Founders as victims of colonialism had little use for state controls or favoritism. Although they were acquainted with Smith's doctrines, their observations on the new Republic and its proposed Constitution in the *Federalist* papers say little about economics, other than advancing property as a countervailing political power.[7] Left to their own devices, Smith noted, businessmen will always gravitate towards profit through the nearest means at hand.

In the first Steamboat Case (1824), Marshall and his Court sat in judgment on the constitutionality of a monopoly granted by the New York State legislature. The beneficiary was Robert Livingston, a prominent New Yorker and powerful politician, who as chancellor of New York had administered the oath of office to President Washington. He was also a born capitalist, with long-term visions of steam-navigation accelerating trade and travel on America's lakes and river systems, joined by canals and bringing western goods to the Atlantic ports. The legislators made the twenty-year monopoly conditional on demonstration that the proposed steamboat could navigate upstream against the Hudson River current at four miles per hour – amidst laughter, it was reported. In 1801, Jefferson appointed Livingston minister to France, where he helped negotiate the Louisiana Purchase (1803), itself a tremendous prospect for waterways transportation on the Mississippi. In Paris he met Robert Fulton, a young Philadelphia inventor and adventurer, intent on selling Napoleon a steam-propelled device for blowing up enemy vessels. The demonstration on the Seine failed, but Livingston and Fulton became partners in planning a steamboat for the New York monopoly. They ordered a 24-horsepower engine from James Watts' factory in England, where Fulton went to sell the Admiralty submersible weapons to use against Napoleon. Unsuccessful, he returned to America, received his shipment and in 1807 launched the Clermont, which made the New York-Albany trip in 35 hours, at 4.7 miles per hour, against the four days required for sailing sloops on the same route.

By 1810, three Fulton steamboats were plying the New York harbor, collecting tribute from interlopers and engendering retaliatory laws from neighboring states. Thomas Gibbons, a rival operator, decided to challenge the monopoly as unconstitutional and sued Aaron Good, now representing the Livingston stake. Gibbons' determination was matched by a cabin-boy promoted to youthful master of a Gibbons ferryboat, Cornelius J. Vanderbilt, who hid in a secret closet when process servers attempted to enforce collection, and later as a railroad tycoon adopted the title Commodore. The New York courts upheld the monopoly and Gibbons appealed to the Supreme Court.

* * *

It is tempting to linger on the rampant capitalism of an earlier America, just as it is to savor the drama of the great cases. The Court does not dispatch legislation or remove it from the books. It hears the cases of individuals, for the most part, who feel their constitutional rights have been violated. Whether the Court agrees or disagrees, it rules so in relation to these individuals. In effect, a principle is established that hereafter other American individuals in similar circumstances can expect similar treatment in any court until the law is amended or the Court reverses itself. The process gives mythic significance to the narratives preceding the hearings, and to the Dred Scotts and Jane Roes who often lend their names to the cases.[8]

The great economic cases, like the civil rights cases, become legendary, correcting the time lag between the law, by its nature deliberate and conservative, and constantly changing social reality. In turn, they generate additional statutes and agencies, as reform-minded legislatures and politicians seize the constitutional opening. The watershed New Deal legislation, which greatly shaped regulated capitalism as we know it today, was confirmed by the Court only after relentless rejections of F.D.R.'s early program. The Court's turn to approval was no doubt influenced by the President's reassuring turn to pragmatic reform rather than a highly-centralized structural change for the economic system, but the resolution was legitimating. Using hypothetical examples, a libertarian would not today consider appealing to the Court on grounds that the mandatory Social Security Act deprived him of the right to do his own pension-planning; nor would

89

a Wall Street executive appeal on grounds that the Securities Exchange Acts violated the rights of investment bankers to keep their own house in order. Either the Court would refuse to hear the cases, or the interests involved would accept their futility, given the power of the major cases. The cases become part of the traditions and expectations needed for private sector planning and are not easily reversed. During his televised Senate Judiciary Committee hearings, Judge Bork patiently lectured the nation on the respect the Court pays to established precedents, referring to the doctrine of *stare decisis*, a disposition to let such decisions stand. The reverse side is the Court's historic tendency to preserve anachronisms, symbolized in the *Dred Scott, Plessy* v. *Ferguson* (equal but separate education), and *Lochner* (maximum work-week) cases.

With these observations in mind, we can view the Court as an analogue of how government institutions – the Court, Congress and Presidency, along with mediating institutions such as the press, organized religion and the intellectual establishment – have restrained dominant capitalism and held it responsible for the common good.[9] The tension, sometimes the conflict, between the opposing forces, is not uneven. Capitalism, alert to change and reform, can hold its own against the institutions. After all, capitalism is where the distribution of money and material satisfactions reside. So long as it efficiently delivers these goods to more and more people, measured by some moral criterion, such as fairness, it should survive with our gratitude. This is not to gainsay the abundant cultural discontents of both freedom and capitalism, which are not the subject of this book. Nor should we avoid less optimistic considerations concerning the future of democratic capitalism, to be discussed in Chapter 7.

* * *

Back to *Gibbons* v. *Ogden*. Chief Justice Marshall, dominating the Court by the force of his intellect and persuasive abilities, faced a dilemma. He was a strong believer in the sanctity of contracts. The Constitution itself had a contract clause, Article I, Section 10 [1], that declared no state shall 'pass any law impairing the obligation of contracts.' It was common knowledge that the clause had been inserted in the final draft by Gouverneur Morris, an arch-conservative who headed the Committee assigned that task, and that it was adopted without notice. The clause suited the Marshall Court. In 1819, in the Dartmouth College case, it reversed New Hampshire legislation that had converted Dartmouth from a private to a state institution, on grounds of contract violation of the charter, as argued by Daniel Webster on behalf of Dartmouth. The protection of contracts, advanced by property interests from the time of the Roman Republic as defense against debt repudiation, was firmly echoed by its American successor. To the Founders' credit, the Congress of 1789 assumed the $77 million of war and other debts of both the states and the Continental Congress, even though they had been largely repudiated or sold at a discount to speculators. The injunction to do so had been stipulated in the Constitution (Article VI, [1]).

Now Marshall was faced with a request to abrogate the monopoly charter, in effect a contract with a limited time span, comparable to restrictive patents that encouraged trade and invention. Concentrating on the necessity of a unified nation without trade barriers among the states, he came down firmly on the anti-monopoly side, finding his justification in the Commerce Clause, in which Congress was empowered to 'regulate commerce with foreign nations, and among the several States, and with the Indian tribes.' Marshall's interpretation extended the federal authority to mean *interstate* commerce, using as an example a foreign nation's shipment headed for a destination that required river passage through several other states. If Congress had power to regulate commerce with foreign nations, such power could not be curbed by states claiming intrastate powers to regulate their internal commerce. The implication that the states had no such powers at all, which they could need for local pilotage regulation, for example, was temporarily avoided by the Court's ruling that since Gibbons had a federal coastal-trade charter, the charter prevailed under the Supremacy Clause of the Constitution, (Article VI, 2), over state restrictions. The double-edged decision ended the monopoly.[10] Within two years steamboats in the New York harbor increased from six to forty-three, and the Mississippi and other key rivers were opened to free passage of steam vessels.

It was not until 1851, sixteen years after Marshall's regime, that a second Steamboat Case, *Cooley v. Board of Court Wardens*, resolved the unsatisfactory division of regulatory authority. Cooley, master of a foreign trade vessel, refused to pay a penalty for violating a Pennsylvania pilotage law on the grounds that the 1824 case determined only federal and not state powers could be exerted on interstate or foreign commerce. The Court ruled there was room for both powers, depending on the subject of regulation, and pilotage was a matter best left to the states, absent any federal claims. Marshall's invention of judicial review was thus improved, step by step, for economic interests, interpreting the spare words of the Founders into becoming an instrument of effective regulation, balancing local interests with the overarching concern for an open, national market.

The underlying significance was the recognition of the need for regulation of economic activity, even in the age of laissez-faire. The Commerce Clause became the workhorse and justification for a myriad of laws and regulatory commissions, both state and federal, embracing practically all areas of economic activity. Granted federal supremacy and national markets – and not the survival of capitalism – were Marshall's objectives, the gradual emergence of regulated capitalism had its roots in the early Court decisions, however providential. The present claims for deregulation should be seen in this context.

The Grain Elevator Case

The Court's school for capitalism in the pre-New Deal era was further called on for the establishment of a public interest priority in the area of regulation. By 1865, large-scale industry, accelerated by technology and the profit-making from war production, had changed America's economic order. The penalties as well as rewards of unrestrained growth drew their toll. Dangerous, long work-weeks, financial panics, poverty, repressive strikes, crowded cities – these are well-known, as are the unprecedented opportunities to rise upward. Less recognized is that among the business establishment itself, inequities of power demanded redress. Antagonisms arose between agricultural and industrial interests, railroads and shippers, farmers and bankers, all holding the Supreme Court in mind as their agency of last resort.

92

Munn & Scott operated a Chicago grain elevator. An 1871 Illinois statute established a maximum charge for storing grain in a public elevator at two cents a bushel. Munn & Scott ignored the law and were charged with the crime of violating it. When the Illinois courts ruled against them, they appealed to the Supreme Court, claiming that a person could not be deprived of liberty and property under the relatively new, post-Civil War antislavery Fourteenth Amendment and its Due Process Clause. That Munn & Scott was a partnership was not a problem, as even corporations had been transformed into 'persons' by laissez-faire Courts anxious to accommodate business interests. The harder question was whether the freedom to charge whatever the market would bear for public storage was a matter of liberty and property, to be protected against the State of Illinois. Then as now, the meaning of the words 'due process' was vague, but assuming the statute was duly passed, the case became a matter of protecting liberty and property for the partners or upholding regulation when the facts indicated a possible stranglehold on farmers by grain-elevator operators in Illinois. A line had to be drawn between a businessman's rights and the common good. Chief Justice Waite granted that liberty and property had broad meaning in the Constitution, but ruled that since Munn & Scott's property was engaged in public use, it must submit to public control when the operator had a virtual monopoly, assuming the state legislature had checked its facts correctly. Justice Stephen J. Field dissented on behalf of free markets. If a legislature can fix the price of one's property, he stated, under the cover of the facts, then anything 'from a calico gown to a city mansion' might be next.[11] Justice Field's dissent became the dominant philosophy of the Court until the New Deal period, when the logic of *Munn* v. *Illinois* prevailed once again, and sociological information as well as facts were accepted.

Notes

1 *National Labor Relations Board* v. *Jones & Laughlin Steel Corp.* 301 U.S. I (1937).

2 *Lochner* v. *New York* 198 U.S. (1905).

3 The 'Takings Clause' of the Fifth Amendment ('nor shall private property
be taken for public use, without just compensation') is a property-
protection device. Although the clause has been interpreted by the Court
to allow widespread appropriation of property for public parks and environmental use, the original emphasis, under Madison's leadership, was
to protect property from the whims of a democratic majority. Similarly, in
the political structure, the Senate was conceived as a safeguard for property rights and given superior status. Comment on the implications of the
Founders' property bias now covers a wide spectrum, well beyond the
materialist 'economic interpretation' of the Constitution by Charles A.
Beard (1913), which excited a previous generation. Many support the
notion that property is a touchstone against which two rival constitutional
visions, self-government (democracy) and limited government (property
rights), contend. The equilibrium worked, enabling unmatched economic
growth, but it is asserted the ghost of Madison's concern now prevents
popular, unpropertied participation in democracy. See Jennifer Nedelsky,
*Private Property and the Limits of American Constitutionalism: The
Madisonian Framework and Its Legacy* (Chicago: The University of
Chicago Press, 1990). J.G.A. Pocock, as noted *supra*, Chapter 3, n. 9, de-
mythologizes the influence of property among the Founders. He proposes
instead a motivating inheritance of republican statecraft, originating in the
Greek *polis*, reborn in Machiavellian Italy, heightened by the Commonwealth revolt, then carried to the American Revolution. The republican
revival enlists a distinguished school in legal studies, headed by Frank
Michelman of Harvard and Cass Sunstein of the University of Chicago.
Both note the obsolescent property balance and seek a renewal of republican deliberative discourse on the level of the Federalist papers. Property
rights should be regarded as political rights (Michelman), and Court
supremacy modified by improved Congressional deliberation (Sunstein).
Bruce Ackerman, currently the most provocative commentator on the
Constitution, downgrades property sentiment among the Founders,
awarding priority to innovative political and moral convictions. He finds
the consensual, popular impulse of 'We the People', also attributed to
Madison, resurrected in the great constitutional changes following the
Civil War and during the New Deal, and would like to see such
'transformative' impulses kept alive. See Bruce Ackerman, *We the
People: Foundations* (Cambridge: Harvard University Press, 1991),
32–57, 81–105. Finally, the Revolutionary historian Gordon S. Wood has
produced a revision of the mainstream evaluation of property used in my

text. He questions dominant property influence by describing a Founding society moving from hierarchy towards equality, in which a large segment of three million citizens view property and wealth as available to all through merit and hard work. See Gordon S. Wood, *The Radicalization of the American Revolution*, (New York: Alfred A. Knopf, 1992). My own intent is to review capitalism's reform concretely and historically as effected by Court and Constitution. Even here theory is implicit. It is the 'legal realism' of men like Justice Holmes and Federal Judge Learned Hand, who venerate the Constitution as a kind of sacred instrument, incrementally rising to the occasion over the years in the hands of wise, independent judges such as themselves, creative but also mindful of their predecessors as they make their interpretations. See Archibald Cox, *The Court and the Constitution*, (Boston: Houghton Mifflin Company, 1987), for a fine summary in this vein by a law professor, practitioner before the Court, and participant in the process which induced a President to resign rather than challenge the Constitution's 'rule of law'.

4 F.A. Hayek, *Capitalism and the Historians* (Chicago: University of Chicago Press, 1954).

5 *McCullough* v. *Maryland* also helped establish judicial supremacy. Additionally, in the Marshall period, *Martin* v. *Hunter's Lessee*, 7 Cranch 603 (1813); Wheat. 304 (1816), helped establish judicial review.

6 A self-serving status designation between property-owners and slave-owners was promoted by the Southern Founders. During the Colonial period, aristocratic plantation owners fostered solidarity between themselves and ordinary farm-owners on grounds that 'both were equal in not being slaves', an alliance lasting through the Civil War. See Edmund S. Morgan, *American Slavery, American Freedom: The Ordeal of Virginia* (New York: W.W. Norton, 1975), 381. The invidious distinction against slaves also served to reassure marginal whites and immigrants in the pre-Civil War North that they too were beneficiaries of 'American equality'. See David Brion Davis, 'The American Dilemma', *New York Review of Books*, 16 July 1992.

7 See Morton White, *Philosophy, the Federalist and the Constitution* (New York: Oxford University Press, 1987), 61–5.

8 The Jane Roe of *Roe* v. *Wade* (1973) is Norma McCorvey, indicating a previous state of reticence about abortion.

9 Note should be taken here of the importance of the media in establishing

a new dialogue between Court and public. The rehabilitation of the Court, after its castigation in the New Deal period, centered on Justice Holmes, a man of infinite glamour and presence, portrayed heroically on stage and in biographies. Since then the drama of the civil rights cases and the moral dilemma of *Roe* v. *Wade* have created an intense, informed interest in the Court, enabling the public to constantly assess each member's place on the liberal-conservative scale, the process intensified by televised Senate confirmation hearings and speculation on the politicization of appointments. The bicentennial of the ratification of the Bill of Rights in 1991 took the nation to school on the Constitution. Coincident with these developments has been the emergence of top-flight Court journalists, such as Anthony Lewis of the *New York Times*, author of *Gideon's Trumpet* and *Make No Law: The Sullivan Case and the First Amendment*, David G. Savage of *The Los Angeles Times*, author of books on the Burger and Rehnquist Courts, Lincoln Caplan of *The New Yorker Magazine*, L. Gordon Crovitz of *The Wall Street Journal*, and Fred Friendly, Nina Totenberg and Roger Mudd of public TV. The law school professors and law review journals continue to examine Court decisions and produce scholarly, conflicting theories of constitutionalism, but the public need for good journalism on the subject is well-served. On the other hand, efforts to conduct a dialogue on constitutional reform itself, to be achieved through Article V's constitutional convention process, have met with supreme indifference on the public's part. Headed by distinguished scholars such as James MacGregor Burns, concerned with the gridlock of checks and balances, they propose structural reforms, including party reforms, to enable governing efficiency on the British cabinet model. See James MacGregor Burns, *The Crosswinds of Freedom* (New York: Alfred A. Knopf, 1989), 647–50.

10 *Gibbons* v. *Ogden*, 9 Wheat. 1 (1824).

11 *Munn* v. *Illinois*, 94 U.S. 113 (1877).

6 The Court and capitalism: the Progressive and New Deal periods

1 The Court in the Progressive Period

Justice Field's laissez-faire doctrine prevailed in the Court for over thirty years, but was circumvented by antitrust legislation and regulatory agency expansion in the Progressive era Presidencies of Theodore Roosevelt, Taft and Wilson. Roosevelt and Wilson, though adversaries, shared a belief in central government as the instrument of national economic reform, and Taft, a firm conservative in other matters, carried on as T.R.'s disciple. The combination of energetic Presidential leadership and a confirming Court moderated capitalism at a peak period of its ideological supremacy and corresponding business power. That no major economic crisis impelled the reforms makes them all the more noteworthy as precursors of New Deal legislation.

The Progressive movement was a phenomenon of enlightened conservatism. Men and women who considered themselves the best and brightest of their generation, by virtue of education and dedication to the public good, identified the political corruption and slums in the cities, and the uneven rewards and harsh working conditions of the new industrial order, as injustices amenable to regulation. It was an optimistic reform movement within the capitalist system, stimulated by investigative journalism and marked by a high degree of moral content. Its unifying strand was a genuine concern about the inability of individual workers and consumers to stand up to the unprecedented powers of large-scale industry. Its arena was basically that of municipal and state reform, but its national targets were 'the malefactors of great wealth', T.R.'s aristocratic put-down for the class he rarely found likeable. Corporate executives and their allies among bankers, lawyers, judges, and laissez-faire professors in the great universities might agree about the municipal corruption, but the thought of government intervention in their preserve was anathema.

With McKinley's assassination in 1901, the 42-year old T.R. became President. Immensely gifted and self-confident, he responded to the Progressive agenda, promising a 'Square Deal', in which the unequal economic factors would be adjusted. T.R. had no illusions about the Supreme Court. For decades the Justices had invalidated state laws enacting business restraints with monotonous regularity, interpreting the Commerce Clause, the Contract Clause, and the Fourteenth Amendment Due Process Clause as walls of protection for employers. In 1902 Roosevelt appointed the 61-year old Oliver Wendell Holmes to the Court, calling him from Massachusetts where Holmes had been Chief Justice. Holmes had already achieved international recognition from his publications and law professorship at Harvard. It is a measure of his discomfort with his new colleagues to note that from 1902 to 1932, when he retired, he had dissented in 43 of 171 cases in which the Court had invalidated state laws. Holmes was by nature conservative, but his concept of law related to experience, not to rigid rules or an economic doctrine unresponsive to social needs.[1] From this vantage, he preferred to sustain the majoritarian legislation of the states, regarding such statutes as closer to the give-and-take of the market world. *Lochner* v. *New York* (1905) concerned a small bakery owner in Utica, New York, who asked the Court to reverse a $50 fine imposed for violating the state's sixty-hour workweek law, on grounds of deprivation of liberty without due process. Justice Peckham, speaking for the Court, combined the notions of liberty and contract into 'liberty of contract' for either side to purchase or sell labor, absent threats to safety, health and public morals, not evidenced in a sixty-hour week. The statute was 'meddlesome' and declared unconstitutional. Holmes' powerful dissent, quoted in Chapter 5, eventually won the day, and 'Lochnerism' became a metaphor for judicial activism against social and economic reforms.

The momentum for economic reform continued, alive in states like Wisconsin, where Governor Robert M. La Follette had launched the

Progressive movement, the Populist tradition, the press and mass circulation magazines, and among a broad public segment. Holmes was not isolated in the Court. A colleague, the first Justice Harlan, had irately dissented over the reversal of a federal income tax act in 1895, and had been the sole dissenter in *Plessy* v. *Ferguson* in 1896.[2] Lochner had been decided by only a 5–4 majority, and in *Mueller* v. *Oregon* (1908), the majority upheld a state law limiting the working hours of women.

The Oregon case links the Progressive era to another independent-minded Justice, appointed by Wilson to the Court in 1916. Louis D. Brandeis, a prominent Boston corporation lawyer devoted to public service causes, won the case for Oregon by introducing overwhelming medical and safety testimony. Acclaimed nationally for his denunciations of large trusts, as business combinations were then called, and of the misuse of 'other people's money' by the financiers, Brandeis influenced T.R.'s initial 'trust-busting' phase. The President soon acknowledged the inevitability and national value of large-scale enterprise, and returned to the Progressive pattern of constructive regulation rather than the Brandeis path of dissolution. In this stance, he was joined by Wilson and the latter's 'New Freedom' program. Their successful efforts, along with those of Taft, were confirmed or left unchallenged by the Court.

The Sherman Anti-Trust Act of 1890, inspired in part by the Steamboat Monopoly Cases, had been rendered dormant by previous administrations and by a Court ruling in 1895 declaring the Act inapplicable to manufacturing combinations. The new President promptly filed a federal suit to break up a northwestern railroad monopoly and was upheld by the Court in *Northern Securities Co.* v. *United States* (1903). T.R. also moved against the meatpacking, oil, and tobacco monopolies, among others. The Court sustained the Administration in every case, including revision of the prior exclusion of manufacturing. In 1903 Roosevelt persuaded Congress to establish a Bureau of Corporations, aimed at illegal business practices, a device for keeping business in line later exerted by Congressional Committees such as Senator Black's on utility company lobbying and Senator Truman's on war contracts, in the F.D.R. administration. After his landslide election victory in 1904, the President challenged the nation's most powerful and visible industry, pressing for national regulation of interstate railroad rates, uncontrolled since the Court's sabotage of the Interstate Commerce Commission in the 1880s. Overcoming Congressional resistance – the 'railroad Senators' were immune from popular election until 1913 – T.R.'s Hepburn Act was a personal triumph, followed by Meat Inspection and Pure Food and Drug Acts, all countenanced by the born-again Court. Under the generally reactionary Taft, antitrust prosecutions continued to be vigorously pursued, and the Mann-Elkins Act of 1910 revived the moribund Interstate Commerce Commission.

President Wilson, a former Governor and university professor of jurisprudence and political economy, lent a firm hand to capitalism's entry into the twentieth century. The Clayton Act of 1914 expanded antitrust activity, including an exemption from antitrust charges (conspiracy in restraint of trade) for labor unions, opening the door to collective bargaining power that would become operative in the New Deal. In the Progressive tradition, Wilson then added more regulation, the Federal Trade Commission, in 1914, authorized to bring antitrust offenders to the Supreme Court if necessary, and to police false advertising. For those concerned with where all this regulation will end, some comfort may be taken by noting that antitrust is now largely a bipartisan orphan, diminished by new economic realities, first, the self-destructing bankruptcies of large-scale organizations crushed by their own weight, and second, the counter-threat from a type of 'industrial policy', which permits combinations aimed at strategic international trade supremacy, alleged to be the specialty of Japan. As for regulatory commissions, the Republican Party Convention Platform of 1992 called for the elimination of the venerable, railroad-oriented Interstate Commerce Commission, perhaps with justification, inasmuch as the Commerce Clause, legitimated by the great Court cases, enables Congress to reach into practically any area of the nation's economy as needed.

Wilson's showpiece was the Federal Reserve Act of 1913, a radical enactment for banking and monetary reform, enabling banking reserves to be moved regionally from cities to farmland, creating the new federal reserve notes we carry in our pockets, and providing a pool of credit for 'monetary policy' efforts to moderate capitalism's chronic ailment, the business cycle. As a footnote to Wilson's economic administration, note must also be taken of a modest clause in his free-trade Underwood Tariff Act of 1913, implementing a federal income tax.[3] The rates were so low as to defy description, but the significance is momentous. Income taxation, whatever the rates, is the keystone for the redistribution of wealth which enables a capitalist country to contemplate social justice in return for the inequalities of the market system. The concept of big government providing big services, including the safety net for those outside the taxable-income group, and for those receiving universally-desired entitlements such as Social Security benefits, depends on massive, involuntary transfer payments from one group to another. The alternative, for command economies, is low taxes, cradle-to-grave security, and everyone on the government payroll. This offer is strong medicine, understandably reviving in present-day Russia nostalgia for its relative order and stability, as that nation struggles towards a capitalist, market system.

In summary, the Progressive era was a landmark in capitalism's maturation, an example of successful institutional reform that lasted until the country was swept into World War I. For the Court's role, the period offers two conclusions. First, the traditional history of the Court as a forty-year captive in the wilderness of laissez-faire ideology prior to the New Deal is clearly overstated. Second, the traditional history of the Court as being concerned, from Marshall's time onward, with only two major problems, federalism versus state sovereignty, and private rights versus the public good, should be revised to include a third area, the Court's involvement with the reform of capitalism.

2 The Court and the New Deal

Franklin D. Roosevelt and the New Deal combine the Presidency with economic policy to a degree unmatched in American history. Additionally, no administration's economic affairs have been so thoroughly documented, commensurate with the great stakes at risk.

From this perspective, historians often highlight The First One Hundred Days (1933) and The Second One Hundred Days (1935) of the New Deal. In tracing capitalism's reform, we will concentrate on legislation passed in these time-frames, resulting in cases in which the Court acted first as the New Deal's nemesis and then as its legitimator. Finally, we will consider the unresolved question, did F.D.R. 'save' capitalism?

The legendary First One Hundred days are well-known. The President was inaugurated on March 4, 1933 in the midst of an unprecedented crisis of failed banks and widespread state bank closings, including New York's on March 3, when $100 billion worth of gold was withdrawn from the banking system. Assembling his cabinet on March 5, Roosevelt obtained approval to close all banks under a 1917 war-powers act relating to raids on gold. On March 6, he declared a 'bank holiday', the psychologically-correct phrase in use for such action. Congress was reconvened by the President for special session on March 9 and within eight hours passed an Administration banking bill preventing gold-hoarding and exporting, and providing for the reopening, with sick banks placed in the hands of conservators. On Sunday night, March 12, a confident, serene President, in a 'fireside chat' over the nation's radios, explained what he had done, person to person, and urged everyone to march into their banks the next morning and accept paper money, not convertible into gold. The magic worked. The stock market rose on Wednesday and a government bond issue was oversubscribed. True, a third of a nation, out of work and hungry, had little business to do with banks, but the national paralysis of fear and inaction had been broken.

Magician, improvisor, lion and fox – all apply to the President judged by history to have been the right man at the right time, in economic as well as actual warfare. Economically, F.D.R. subscribed to no doctrine. His background was conservative, including a period as business executive and entrepreneur, but his temperament was experimental and risk-taking, willing to play the percentages and acknowledge error. For consistency, his economic decisions were basically grounded in a strong faith in democracy, and a sense of compassion and urgency regarding human suffering.

The inconsistency of such formulation is revealed in the Economy Act obtained from Congress as his next legislation, two days later. Inherited from his recent campaign rhetoric and reflecting his sense of obligation to such promises, it was also an overture to his powerful opponents in the business world. The legislation was a mix of cost reductions, involving all federal salaries, including those of Congress, and authority to reduce veterans' pensions, as a first step toward reducing the $5 billion national debt. Otherwise the government was on the road to bankruptcy, F.D.R. sententiously warned. When Congress later regained its composure, all the items were legislated out. Equally trivial, 3.2 beer and light wines were legislated a few days later, in anticipation of reversing the Prohibition Amendment.

Immensely important economic bills, however, were enacted in The Hundred Days, all candidates for invalidation by the Supreme Court, once the grace period of emergency had expired. The legislation included comprehensive agricultural support, massive home and farm mortgage bailouts, a banking act introducing deposit insurance, a securities regulation act, regional power development, departure from the deflationary gold standard, and the launching of the ill-fated NIRA (administered by the NRA), a far-reaching, two-year 'industrial recovery act', aimed at inflating prices, stabilizing production and regulating business practices.

A notable exception to escape the Court gauntlet was a national federal emergency relief act passed in the Hundred Days, followed by emergency public employment projects initiated early in 1934 (Civilian Works Administration) and 1935 (Works Progress Administration and Public Works Administration), dispensed by the redoubtable Harry Hopkins and Harold Ickes. The Court, though occupied by four adamant Justice Field adherents, did not entertain challenges to this unprecedented exercise of federal power, sharing the national recognition of its necessity.

In passing, note should be taken of its parameters. Including the Civilian Conservation Corps and National Youth Administration programs, over three to four millions were on the public rolls from 1933 to 1938, out of a population of 125 million compared with today's 250 million. The unemployed not covered by government shelters ranged from over twelve million in 1933 to about seven million when recovery was insured by preparation for World War II. Altogether it was a decade of resigned acceptance no longer to be counted on by the custodians of American capitalism. Nor need it be, given our consensus for permanent Social Security, bank deposit insurance, and flexible unemployment insurance as shock-absorbers for recession, let alone depression.

The Works Progress Administration of Harry Hopkins received the major share of funds and was the largest employer, though restrained by the Administration's conservative provision that it could not perform work ordinarily provided by the private sector. Hence the perennial criticism that it engaged in leaf-raking and arts projects contrived by the ingenious Hopkins. Although it paid only token wages, the WPA did not require a means test, as did outright relief, and millions of former middle-class family heads gratefully accepted the occupational and psychological benefits of compensated work. F.D.R. himself, imbued with the Protestant ethic of an honest day's work, regarded all the works projects as dole, and was anxious to end them. Still, when he proposed a $5 billion appropriation for the work and relief agencies in 1934, passed early in 1935, it was the largest governmental expenditure in recorded history. For an example of how permanent the so-called welfare state has become in capitalist countries since the New Deal, consider, even with inflationary adjustments, Japan's proposed $100 billion public works project of 1993, at prevailing wages, initiated in response to unemployment of less than 3 per cent, an overextended financial system, and infrastructure in need of renovation.

* * *

On Black Monday, May 27, 1935, the Supreme Court convened to announce its decision on a key NRA case. F.D.R. and his legal advisors, including Harvard law professor Felix Frankfurter, a White House confidante, had grave uncertainties about the Court. Justices McReynolds, Sutherland, Van Devanter and Butler were tenacious anti-New Dealers. The highly respected Chief Justice, Charles Evans Hughes, a former Republican candidate for President, superbly equipped by background and intelligence for his position, preferred a mask of neutrality. The aging Brandeis, the scholarly Cardozo, appointed by Hoover, and the broad-gauged Harlan Fiske Stone were authentic 'liberals'. Owen Roberts, also appointed by Hoover, was the youngest at fifty-eight. Holmes, idolized by F.D.R., had retired in 1932. After F.D.R.'s inauguration, the President called on the 92-year old Holmes, his cousin's appointee.

If either Hughes or Roberts joined the conservative four, New Deal legislation faced invalidation as unconstitutional. There were hopeful signs. In January 1934, a 5–4 decision written by Hughes upheld a Minnesota mortgage moratorium act, justifying the contract abrogation on grounds of emergency. New Deal legislation had been sprinkled with emergency preambles. In March 1934, a 5–4 decision written by Roberts sustained New York state regulation of retail milk prices. In January 1935 the first federal statute reached the Court, in which a poorly drawn oil industry provision of the NRA was invalidated. Next a February 1935 case presented a close call for the Administration. A 5–4 decision ruled that although the repudiation of the gold clause in government bonds was 'immoral' as well as unconstitutional, bondholders nevertheless could not sue for recovery. The majority, fearing financial chaos, had been forced to neglect an apparent duty. Court-watchers sensed the possibility of revenge.

In 1934, the Schechter brothers, Brooklyn poultry wholesalers, were convicted of violating the wage and hour provisions of the NRA Live Poultry Code, and selling diseased chickens to boot. On Black Monday, the Court rendered a 9–0 decision that struck down the entire National Industrial Recovery Act. The delegation of legislative powers to code-makers, however voluntary their association, was 'delegation running riot', declared Cardozo. Furthermore, the Court added, Schechters' business was done in New York State only; hence the Commerce Clause as foundation was inapplicable. Such a narrow interpretation of the clause, which Holmes had labored to liken to the flow of a river, doomed national application of the act.

The NRA had already achieved substantial gains and enthusiasm, and was about to expire in June. It might have passed the Court as a revised act, but its proliferation under the hectic General Hugh Johnson had produced a bureaucratic maze incompatible with America's traditional preference for decentralized capitalism, short of wartime claims. F.D.R., ever the realist, held an urbane press conference the next day and asked how any kind of economic legislation could withstand such a Commerce Clause interpretation. He labelled the Court a 'horse and buggy' institution and left the nation awaiting his next move.

* * *

Two years after his mandate, F.D.R. had lost momentum. The new Congress, though solidly Democratic, was splintered and rebellious. F.D.R.'s January 1935 proposal to join the World Court was defeated by the isolationist wing, the antics of Father Coughlin, and an unfriendly press. The US Chamber of Commerce, a warm backer at the outset, now turned vehemently against the New Deal, one of several messages indicating F.D.R.'s hopes for a business coalition were fragile. Additionally, the revival of national political energy spawned rival economic prophets, Dr. Francis Townsend, Huey Long and Father Coughlin.

The paranoid streak in American politics described by the historian Richard Hofstadter has a distinct economic coloration – silver fanatics, goldbugs, farmers against city people and their villainous bankers, all venting sufficient logic to generate a whirlwind of followers. F.D.R. himself played the game, denouncing economic royalists and pledging to expel moneychangers from the temple. Now an assorted trio of experts were stealing the headlines and diminishing his leadership.

Against traditional capitalism and the vested interests as well as the New Deal, their demand was for quicker and larger prescriptions. Dr. Townsend was benign in such company. He recognized a genuine constituency of older people, cast-off and fearful. The Administration had announced plans for old-age security, but they lacked priority and concerned modest payments ten years down the road. The Townsend Plan called for a grandiose minimum of $200 monthly for the un-employed over 65, funded by a vague sales tax, with each recipient pledged to spend it all in the next month in the United States, thereby generating purchasing power. Townsend clubs flourished and expired in due course, but the upright doctor, though economically primitive, was headed in the right direction. Long, the Louisiana Senator, was a malevolent regional Populist, swaggering and corrupt, demanding a spurious 'Share Our Wealth' program. He was planning a dictatorial third party, hopefully with Coughlin and Townsend support, when

106

assassinated on the State House steps in Baton Rouge in September 1935, age 42.

In retrospect, Father Coughlin, because of his communication skills and superior intellect, would have been a genuine threat to democratic capitalism, had he found more reputable political allies. It can happen here, as Sinclair Lewis wrote in 1935, and Coughlin's brief comet, along with F.D.R.'s patient decision to wait him out, are lessons for later generations. An Orwellian prototype, Coughlin was a master of the radio media. He demonstrated power to move millions toward his benevolent-sounding National Union for Social Justice, a man of the church harping on arcane money matters to a nation bereft of money. The Radio Priest dated back to the Hoover administration, against which he had preached before endorsing and then rejecting the New Deal. The significance of Father Coughlin lay in the sustained number of his followers, a weekly audience for years on the CBS national network of forty million listeners. Less measurable were his mail claims, but historians assert he received more mail than anyone in the country, including the President.

His nostrum was a blend of metallic formulas for inducing inflation, laced with vitriolic attacks on bankers as the masters of a sinister capitalist regime. A talent for strange locutions and mellifluousness mesmerized listeners unwilling to identify the message as claptrap. Revalue the gold ounce, remonetize silver, nationalize the banks to end the money shortage – hardly a recipe for weekly radio time without Father Coughlin's demons: bankers and their filthy gold standard revelling in their profits from restricting the flow of goods from the factories and the farms to the people. Finally, 'atheistic capitalism is not worth saving... One way is Christianity; the other way is Bolshevism.' The feat of equating capitalism with communism may have been only a straw reflecting the need for weekly bonfires, in which endeavor Father Coughlin ultimately self-destructed. He not only added a stream of anti-Semitism and pro-Nazism to his message, but, campaigning for William Lemke's third party in the 1936 election, called Roosevelt a liar and identified Secretary of State Cordell Hull and other cabinet members as Communists. The Vatican finally expressed displeasure, and Father Coughlin left the air in the wake of F.D.R.'s resounding victory over Governor Landon.

Pressured by business groups and economic messiahs, F.D.R. now faced the Supreme Court crisis. A possible strategy of Court-packing was deferred until after the 1936 election. Meanwhile, the President exerted his leadership and called for public support by insisting that Congress, about to adjourn in early June 1935, stay in session to complete and pass new legislation, inaugurating The Second One Hundred Days. Four major bills, all passed in this period, can be seen either as a defiant challenge to rising business opposition, spearheaded by the Dupont-led American Liberty League, or as an effort to reform capitalism for its own good.

They included first, passage of the stalled Social Security bill, modest in its initial provisions and far less generous than European statutes of the time, but still a commitment to welfarism as the price to be paid for the inequalities of the economic system, a huge change in American expectations. On the downside, not only were the provisions meager, but F.D.R.'s insistence on employee contributions created an untimely drain on purchasing power for the weak economy. Still, the President's instincts were right: by making the people pay into the plan, he observed they would consider it their own, and the bill could never be taken away from them.[4] The bill also included nationwide unemployment insurance, conservatively allocated to the states for participation and administration. Decentralization, whenever possible, guided by reform statutes and regulations emanating from Washington, reflected Justice Brandeis' persistent influence, symbolized by his rejection of the NRA. It would be the new flag of the Administration, replacing the tentative experiments in a highly-planned economic structure.

Next, a banking bill, led by one of F.D.R.'s business recruits, the Utah banker Marriner Eccles, removed Federal Reserve power from New York to Washington, coordinating banking decisions, and establishing national control over currency and credit. Eccles became chairman of the Fed's Board of Governors, whose members were now protected by fourteen-year terms. His bill had been aided by support from California's A.P. Giannini, like Joseph P. Kennedy, the first SEC Chairman, a link to the business community. As times change, so does the focus of reform. The Fed's problem currently centers on undue influence from Washington, particularly in election years.

A third bill, in the Brandeisian tradition of anti-monopoly, was the Wheeler-Rayburn bill, known for its 'death-sentence' aimed at utility holding companies. Utilities vied with banking institutions for favorite miscreant status in the New Deal world. They were of uncontrollable size, swallowed competition, corrupted legislatures, fleeced consumers, and refused to bring electrification to millions of farm homes. The greatest utility-combiner of all, Chicago's Samuel Insull, had disgraced himself in Hoover's time as a charlatan, fleeing ignominiously to Europe to escape prosecution. Their lobbies were still powerful, especially among House members, and the 'death-sentence' – the one-sided empowerment of the SEC to dissolve any utility 'unable to justify its existence' – sensibly was watered down to insure passage of the bill. Most of the great empires were broken up within three years, and the industry's subjection to the SEC's full-disclosure of financial information actually helped it raise future capital. America's ambivalent relationship with business heroes, shared by F.D.R. himself, was demonstrated by the record of the Republican candidate for the Presidency in 1940, Wendell L. Willkie. Never an office-holder, the 48-year old president of Commonwealth and Southern, a major utility holding company, polled 22 million votes to F.D.R.'s 27 million.

The fourth bill, the National Labor Relations Act, known as the Wagner Act, was a major step in the history of American capitalism because it redressed the balance of power between capital and labor. The concept involved was far more fundamental than the constant efforts of the states to remove the remaining barrier against wage and hour legislation, the Court's Lochnerian contention that both employer and employee still had equal strength to negotiate their contracts. The Wagner Act was a deliberate attempt to advance the cause of unions by giving them a one-way advantage over anti-union employers, declaring that interference with union organization and activity would be considered an unfair labor practice subject to harsh federal sanctions and penalties. Given the global awareness of charges of class-domination, inspired by the theories of Rousseau through

Marx in modern times, alleging a power-relationship reinforced by government, employers understandably sensed a variation of that arrangement, resulting in government-enforced labor domination. It was more than a matter of accepting wage and hour legislation, or of admitting unions restricted to mediating issues like working conditions, which reasonable employers could anticipate as inevitable. The fear of larger employers was loss of power to run their businesses, particularly to hire and fire, regardless of reforms. For labor, at that time relatively non-ideological, there was no ambition to own the forces of production, and little to become a national political party, as on the Continent. America's mild temperament in that direction is evidenced by Willkie's aforementioned 22 million Republican votes in 1940, three years after the sit-down strike in General Motors' Flint, Michigan plant, certainly a multi-class voter turnout. Labor and its supporters in the Administration and Congress were redressing the unfairness of a bitter history of strike repression by police and federal troops, as well as legislating the power and status available through collective strength at the bargaining table. Capitalism was the beneficiary of such a moderate adjustment.

Why then did the Administration fear reversal of the Wagner Act by the Court? A good part of the answer lies in the hold of laissez-faire ideology on the nation, reinforced over three decades by the dominant opinion-makers, judges, bankers, attorneys, business executives, newspaper publishers, and educators, all lagging behind the conservative but realistic Holmes' recognition of 'the felt necessities of the time'. An example would be the venerated William Howard Taft, Circuit Judge, Solicitor General, Secretary of War, President, then Chief Justice of the Court. In that capacity, he acknowledged that unions were essential in an industrial age for laborers to deal on equal terms with employers. Yet he publicly warned, during the 1920 election, that Democratic appointments to the Supreme Court would cause 'Socialistic raids' on property rights.[5] The four die-hards on the New Deal Court were even more immersed in the past and fears of foreign ideology. After the gold-clause case, Justice McReynolds announced: 'As for the Constitution, it does not seem too much to say that it is gone... Shame and humiliation are on us now.'[6] Some tolerance should be reserved for these mind-sets. In a Burkean perspective,

110

the time-lag inherent in the law and its courts brings reform rather than revolution. But at what human cost?

* * *

Industry immediately challenged the Wagner Act by violating it. Approximately two years after its passage, a group of cases testing the authority of the National Labor Relations Board made its way to the Court, involving a clothing manufacturer, a truck-trailer producer, an interstate bus line and the Associated Press. The cases were consolidated under a fifth case, *National Labor Relations Board* v. *Jones & Laughlin Steel Corp.* (1937). Like the other great economic cases cited in our analogue of Court and capitalism, this was a case of individuals, Harry Phillips, Royal Boyer and their friends, requesting a decision on behalf of all other individuals who might face a similar situation.

First, a review of pertinent Court cases since Black Monday in April 1935. Early in 1936, a 6–3 decision invalidated the Agricultural Adjustment Act, like the NRA a major act of the First Hundred Days, directed toward relief of farming families, completely devastated by drought, depression, and low prices.[7] The AAA foundered on the technical item that its processing-tax authority was illegal, but the comprehensive nature of the act, including payment for 'plowing under' crops and decimating animal production, had numbered its days. Congress immediately passed a new farm act, emphasizing payments for soil conservation and crop substitution, believed to be Court-proof, as doubts about Social Security and the Wagner Act intensified. In the spring of 1936, the Guffey Act, a post-NRA attempt to stabilize the soft-coal industry, was invalidated by a 5–4 decision, Justice Roberts supplying the majority vote. Another 5–4 decision, a month later, invalidated a New York state minimum wage law, again with Roberts' support.

In this atmosphere, the adversaries gathered in the great courthouse, only completed in 1935, to hear the narrative and argue the case over a period of three days. John W. Davis, former Solicitor General, ambassador to Great Britain and Democratic candidate for President against Coolidge in 1920, headed the defendants' team of lawyers. The young Charles E. Wyzanski, six years out of Harvard Law, later

111

to become a distinguished federal judge, led the government group. For background, note that independent union activity in the steel industry was virtually dead, crushed by the defeat of its legendary strikes. The success of John L. Lewis' mine workers in the neighboring coal fields, the agony of the depression, and the stimulus of the New Deal had restored life to the movement in Pennsylvania's steel region. In August 1934, the narrative revealed, the venerable Amalgamated Association of Iron and Steel Workers chartered a lodge in the Aliquippa division of Jones & Laughlin, with Harry Phillips, a motor inspector, as president. Aliquippa was a company town, landlord to several hundred dwellings, owner of the street railway and waterworks, and employer of the police force. Phillips had testified to special attention from the police force, ranging from an offer to join the force at higher pay to denial of protection after being beaten up at the company entrance while on the night shift, having been followed to work, he claimed, by a police car. On July 20, 1935, he was summarily fired for too slow a response to a machinery breakdown. Eight other union organizers were similarly ejected, including Royal Boyer who had signed 250 black employees to membership, and Dominic Brandy, a twenty-five year J&L employee who had recruited 665 Italian members.

Two months later, in April 1937, Chief Justice Hughes read the 5–4 opinion against Jones & Laughlin, Justice Roberts again supplying the majority vote, but on the New Deal side. The Commerce Clause was deemed to include any intrastate activities so closely related to interstate commerce that Congress could not be denied their control; nor could 'production' be excluded from the definition of commerce as in previous cases. Finally the disturbances that might flow from union suppression were of sufficient connection with the promotion and regulation of interstate commerce as to justify prohibiting such activity. No more thorough expansion of the Commerce Clause could be wished.

The results of the Jones & Laughlin case were twofold. First the decision was a watershed change in direction for the Court. On March 29, it had already upheld, by a 5–4 decision, Roberts again, a Washington state minimum-wage law, reversing the previous year's New York state decision, and opening the way to the last of the New Deal measures, the Fair Labor Standards Act of 1938.[8] More important, on May 24, the Court confirmed its change of direction with two 5–4 decisions validating the unemployment insurance provisions of the Social Security Act and a 7–2 decision holding old-age pensions as constitutional.

Second, the development allowed F.D.R. to abandon his disastrous Court-packing expedition for which he had practically no support. In short time, his own appointments gave him a distinct majority, but there were few cases to consider as the nation turned to the prospect of World War II.

3 Did F.D.R. Save Capitalism?

Did Roosevelt save capitalism? The question is fallacious – no one saves countries or institutions. My own judgment is that he was a major factor in preserving capitalism, during its ordeal of depression, by taking extraordinary measures to revive the system rather than admit its bankruptcy. This is apparent in such matters as his search for business approval, his decision to reform rather than nationalize the failed banking system, his conservative attitude toward the dole, his cheerful abandonment of the NRA, his insistence on employee Social Security contributions, even his misguided ventures in economizing. In the last capacity, he went personally to Congress to veto the Patman bonus bill (and was overridden) in 1935. If you judge a man by his enemies, Father Coughlin and Huey Long certainly had no use for F.D.R.'s alleged capitalism.

To the extent that F.D.R. subscribed to any economic theory, Brandeis' capitalist creed of anti-monopoly and decentralization for a regulated profit system seemed to capture the Roosevelt of the Second Hundred Days, but F.D.R. was essentially a pragmatist and experimenter, not a true believer. John Maynard Keynes' theory of sustained deficit-spending as the way out of a deflationary depression was not fully comprehended in the early New Deal years, certainly not by Roosevelt as evidenced by his on-again, off-again public works projects. Only a few of those in power, such as Marriner Eccles, were Keynesians by instinct without realizing it.[9] Even so, Keynes was a

113

capitalist, as President Nixon implied when he announced his Keynesian affiliation in 1971. On the watershed Wagner Act, which tipped the power balance between capital and labor, alarming business interests more than any other New Deal legislation, F.D.R. revealed his uncertainty about radical changes. To Senator Wagner's frustration, he (and Secretary of Labor Perkins) initially rejected the bill until 1935, when F.D.R. inexplicably decided to back it.[10] On the other hand, the President saw no contradiction between capitalism and a welfare net.

Judged by his excoriation and taunting of his capitalist critics, symbolized by Al Smith in white tie and tails at the two-thousand dollar plate American Liberty League dinner in Washington in January 1936, F.D.R. was an intemperate rabble-rouser. Yet note his remarks in his second-term campaign speech before 100,000 wildly-cheering fans in the Chicago stadium on October 14, 1936. Rather than dispense class invective, F.D.R. presented his case to the businessmen of America:

> Behind the growing recovery of today is a story of deliberate government acceptance of responsibility to save business, to save the American system of private enterprise and economic democracy... I believe, I have always believed, and I will always believe in private enterprise as the backbone of economic well-being in the United States...The struggle against private monopoly is a struggle for, and not against, American business. It is a struggle to preserve individual enterprise and economic freedom.[11]

It may be more objective to discount F.D.R.'s special pleading and to hear other voices. Most of the powerful and respected business leadership of America, including men like Wendell L. Willkie, regarded the New Deal as a turn away from capitalism towards socialism. This was a far more sophisticated fear than the emotional and selfish reaction of those rejecting F.D.R. because he was 'a traitor to his class', or instigator of the 'Soak the Rich' (William Randolph Hearst's constant refrain) tax act of 1935, involving top tax-rates middle-class Americans would consider a windfall today. Any serious discussion of capitalism versus socialism would have to center on certain structural changes beyond which the systems differ essentially, not items like wage and hour requirements or old-age pensions, long

114

ago established in Bismarck's imperial Germany. It would not even depend on 'private monopoly', which contemporary critics of capitalism like John K. Galbraith reluctantly accept for administered-price, large organizations indispensable to modern industrial states, including democracies.

What then are the bright-line differences then and now? Certainly the structural differences would start with the private ownership of production, for the most part, rather than nationalized ownership, and the profit system, for the most part, identified by a 'free-market' apparatus for establishing costs of labor and capital, and prices of products. On that score, fears might be justified over the NRA and AAA, but hardly over the rest of the New Deal. A major exception would be the massive shift of power between capital and labor anticipated from the Wagner Act. But that may now be seen as an excess of fear on the two sides of the power-equilibrium. Labor saw the shift as essential because of the prior history of collusion between large industrial organizations and federal troops and local police to put down strikes. Granted the Wagner Act was highly desirable, not even President Hoover would likely have countenanced such collusion, more typical of fascism than democratic capitalism. Its day was largely over in America. Employers, on the other hand, seem to have been politically naive, if not excessively fearful. It was evident even then that in a true socialist economy, unions might not flourish, and in centralized distortions of socialism, independent unions had no place. On the record, unions did not take over American industry.[12] There may be rebuttals to this simplification, but it should lend amplification to F.D.R.'s inaugural call: 'The nation has nothing to fear but fear itself.'

The NRA was indeed a turn away from capitalism, not toward socialism as much as to mercantilism, the state-directed version of capitalism perfected by Colbert for Louis XIV, which the NRA's endless codes for quality control and production quotas resembled.[13] It was subject to review after two years and included the first appropriation for public works employment, but once the initial enthusiasm and success had worn off, business interests rightly rejected its bureaucratic overload as an inefficient substitute for market capitalism. They were confirmed in their opinion when even 'old Isaiah', F.D.R.'s favorite name for the righteous Brandeis, joined in the 9–0

115

Court decision. F.D.R., not in thrall to state-planning, realized his emergency experiment could not survive and turned to other strategies. Arthur Schlesinger, Jr., historian of the New Deal, claims the NRA's demise marked the end of the Administration's interest in such planning and its return to the Progressive agenda for reform within the competitive capitalist system. 'I think perhaps NRA has done all it can do,' Secretary Perkins recalls F.D.R. told her, 'I don't want to impose a system on this country that will set aside the anti-trust laws on any permanent basis.'[14] Men like Rexford Tugwell and Hugh Johnson, highly committed to what is now called social-engineering, were no longer prominent in the Administration.[15]

The AAA's rise, fall and restoration is more complex in relation to capitalism. In its original form, it was a mix of financial relief and incentives to curtail production for highly-mortgaged farmers whose over-supply and price dilemmas were resistant to normal capitalist market adjustments. The one thing it did not resemble was the forced collectivization of private farms associated with socialism. Its unique problems are still reflected in bipartisan agricultural budgets of approximately $50 billion annually, including food stamps for 27 million Americans, an accommodation with capitalism that cannot be charged to the New Deal alone. F.D.R.'s concern for the farm population can be seen in context of the '30s, when the farm states were a potent political and symbolic constituency. A landed country squire himself, F.D.R. understood the pain and frustration of this debt-burdened, independent class facing foreclosure on its hard-earned property. He chose Henry A. Wallace, the third generation editor of *Wallace's Farmer*, and son of a Republican Secretary of Agriculture, as his 1936 vice-president, in effect placing a lobbyist for farm interests in the White House. Radical support measures for conservative, property-oriented farmers are commonplace among capitalist nations.

* * *

In summary, F.D.R.'s rendezvous with capitalism makes him look more like a conservator than subverter, confirming his own self-appraisal. Under his leadership, the institutions of Court, Congress, and Presidency combined to reform capitalism in its darkest period.

Notes

1 Oliver Wendell Holmes, Jr. *The Common Law*, Mark Howe, ed. (London, Macmillan, 1968), 5.

2 Justice Harlan's grandson, also Justice John Marshall Harlan, voted with the majority to overthrow Plessy in *Brown* v. *Board of Education*, 347 U.S. 483 (1954).

3 The Sixteenth Amendment (1913) was the ultimate authorization for the income tax. A war-time income tax under President Lincoln was soon overthrown by the Supreme Court.

4 Arthur M. Schlesinger, Jr., *The Coming of the New Deal* (Boston: Houghton Mifflin, 1959), 308–9.

5 Cox, *The Court and the Constitution*, 135.

6 William E. Leuchtenberg, *Franklin D. Roosevelt and the New Deal* (New York: Harper & Row, 1963), 144.

7 *United States* v. *Butler*, 297 U.S. 61 (1936).

8 *West Coast Hotels* v. *Parrish*, 300 U.S. 379 (1937). In this case, the Court moved beyond its old boundary of 'health, safety and morals' to 'the welfare and interests of the community'.

9 Marriner Eccles, *Beckoning Frontiers* (New York: Alfred A. Knopf, 1951), 130–32.

10 Leuchtenberg, *Franklin D. Roosevelt and the New Deal*, 150–51.

11 Arthur M. Schlesinger, Jr., *The Politics of Upheaval* (Cambridge: Houghton Mifflin, 1960), 631-32.

12 The Wagner Act was modified by the Taft-Hartley Labor Act of 1947, passed over President Truman's veto. The Act empowers the government to obtain an 80-day 'cooling-off period', preventing strikes endangering national health and safety, and limits other items such as jurisdictional strikes between unions, but essentially collective bargaining has been preserved.

13 Irving S. Michelman, *The Roots of Capitalism in Western Civilization* (New York: Frederick Fell, 1983), 179–221.

14 Schlesinger, *The Politics of Upheaval*, 289.

15 F.D.R.'s pragmatic turn from the state-planning tendencies of the 'First New Deal' to the regulated capitalism of the 'Second New Deal' has been powerfully stated by Schlesinger, *ibid.*, 389–92, 649–57. Leuchtenberg, *Franklin D. Roosevelt and the New Deal*, sees less of a contrast, but agrees F.D.R. firmly believed in preserving capitalism, 163–65. James Mac-Gregor Burns confirms my summary concerning F.D.R. (Letter to author dated 22 January 1993.)

7 The future of democratic capitalism: two views

1 Schumpeter's Prediction

'Can capitalism survive?' 'No, I do not think it can.'[1] 'Can socialism work?' 'Of course it can.'[2] Joseph Schumpeter's dialogue with himself has entered the archives of Great Questions through his classic, *Capitalism, Socialism and Democracy* (1942), and its confirmation, 'The March into Socialism', an address to the American Economic Association on December 30, 1949, shortly before his death. The prediction came not from an enemy of capitalism, but from an ardent supporter: 'Capitalism... means a scheme of values, an attitude towards life, a civilization – the civilization of inequality and of the family fortune. This civilization is rapidly passing away, however. Let us rejoice or else lament the fact as much as everyone of us likes; but do not let us shut our eyes to it.'[3]

Schumpeter (1883–1950) was considered a genius by many of his peers, impressed by his erudition and articulateness. A Harvard professor, recruited from Austria in 1932, affecting boots and capes, he had been a finance minister and banker, the youngest full professor in the realm, and author of four books and numerous articles before arriving at Cambridge. His early *The Theory of Economic Development*, published in America in 1926, celebrated the entrepreneur as the elite, creative individual who brought life to an otherwise static, 'circular' capitalism. No modern interpreter, save possibly the novelist-cultist Ayn Rand, has seen such romantic, indispensable qualities in the entrepreneur. Schumpeter wrote:

First of all, there is the dream and the will to found a private kingdom... then there is the will to conquer: the impulse to fight, to prove oneself superior to others... Finally, there is the joy of creating.[4]

In the midst of the Great Depression, heroic entrepreneurs, though providing a non-exploitative rebuttal to Marx concerning capitalist motivation, were hardly American icons. Although Schumpeter produced a major work on business cycles and soon became prominent in his profession, he remained enigmatic to his colleagues, most of whom became instant Keynesians in an era of government-intervention enthusiasm.

All took notice of *Capitalism, Socialism and Democracy*, however, as it addressed the question of whether capitalism, having survived the Depression, could make it for the long run. Now Schumpeter's entrepreneur was presented in a tragic as well as heroic light, his superior energizing qualities becoming extinguished by internal rather than external forces.

Although he is still esteemed for his concepts of 'gales of innovation' and 'Creative Destruction', providing new products and markets even as profits fell, this is not the period of Schumpeter's triumph. In making his prediction, he observed that one hundred years, more or less, would constitute the test period. Two recent biographies, a seminar at the University of Notre Dame, now in book form, and a special issue of the *Journal of Democracy*, featuring global contributors, have re-examined Schumpeter on the fiftieth anniversary of his book.[5]

Some of the information, though trivial, is revealing. 'I have three ambitions,' he is quoted, 'to be the greatest economist in the world, the greatest horseman in Austria, and the best lover in Vienna. Well, in one of those goals I have failed.'[6] His psyche has been probed by members of his profession. Peter L. Berger attributes Schumpeter's pessimism to the frequent melancholia, bordering on masochism, of Austrian intellectuals born in the shadow of the Habsburg monarchy, averted by Berger himself.[7] Paul Samuelson has commented: '...his diaries reveal him to have been a seriously depressed personality under the surface... what sophisticated people like Schumpeter should hate to have happen, they paranoidly expect to happen.'[8] Robert Heilbroner, a student at Harvard during Schumpeter's sojourn, introduced him as a disquieting prophet in the first edition of *The Worldly Philosophers*, whose cast ranged from Adam Smith to J.M. Keynes. Schumpeter's question, he noted, was the primary question of the day, but the answer was perplexing, for Schumpeter had diagnosed the death of capitalism from social and not economic illness.[9]

* * *

The entrepreneurial family-firm founder, establishing generational ownership, reflected Schumpeter's unabashed elitism. He must have been aware that competent successors were exceptional, affecting great firms as well as hereditary monarchies, and certainly were not a requirement for capitalism's survival. The disappearance of new founders as a class would present a more serious problem. One can offer current reincarnations of the doomed type, starting with Sam Walton, Ross Perot and Konosuke Matsushita, but Schumpeter uncontradicted is his best rebuttal.

The system Schumpeter saw in decline was one he termed 'unfettered capitalism', specifically unfettered by the state or by treacherous cultural forces. The degree of permissible state intervention reveals how profoundly conservative Schumpeter was by modern standards. He regarded the New Deal skeptically, advising his students that depressions were good therapy.[10] The English and American tax practices, he charged, competed well with Marx's measure of the amount of surplus value being extracted from labor.[11]

Still his analysis of subversion, internal and external, should be heard, if only to caution us about our own certainties. Capitalism's problem, he asserted, derived not from its uncontrolled acquisitive tendency, which bothered Smith and Marx, but from the malaise of its maturity. Internally a structural weakening could be traced to its very success. The system's vitality had been a result of its 'Creative Destruction', a beneficial process generating constant product innovation and providing ever-ready opportunities for new investments, profits, and prosperity, *contra* Marx in that respect. Inevitably the need for research and mass production required large corporate monopolies, or oligopolies, in which personal management was delegated to bureaucratic board rooms and professional managers, a new breed,

121

he confidently asserted, who could function just as well under state ownership, or socialism. The change might be arrested, he stated, were not family values under siege. Not the family values we associate with crime and similar problems, but the expanding bourgeois class, with its debasement of the grand homes of style and refinement once occupied by talented entrepreneurs, whose privacy enabled them to contemplate new adventures and to raise multiple children from whom successors might emerge.[12]

Linked to this internal, structural problem of mature capitalism was an external cultural threat, the subtle opposition of rationality itself. The same rational bent of mind that had nourished the entrepreneurial spirit into creating epochal efficiency and innovation now produced an environment unfriendly to the acquisitive instinct and the profit motive. Schumpeter took seriously, and perhaps personally, the post-Depression rejection of business values and the disposition to redistribute wealth through welfarism displayed by rational intellectuals, including a network within the capitalist class itself. Additionally he believed that capitalists, once able to exert influence on the democratic state, heretofore voluntarily amenable to their interests, simply did not have the talent for democratic politics.[13] Altogether it was a prescription for euthanasia, involving democracy's loss (Schumpeter showed little interest in democracy's potential for reforming and energizing capitalism), and socialism's gain by default.

* * *

Schumpeter's prediction is in shambles due to the demise of socialism in Russia and its East European satellites beginning in 1989. It is not just a matter of holding him accountable, perhaps unfairly, fifty years later and on the occasion of an earth-shaking event as well. Most of the world's experts were caught equally off-base. In retrospect, Schumpeter's analysis and feelings about capitalism and its alternate harbors lack not only cogency but appear mean-spirited as well, certainly about democracy as compared with socialism.

Without Russia's fall, contemporary judgments about the rival economic systems would continue to be largely theoretical. The economy of either Russia or the Republic of China (current population over 1.2 billion) had to fall, or at least stumble grievously, in order to establish the triumph of capitalism, despite the latter's poverty, crime, race problems, crippling deficits, and cycles of serious unemployment. Let us grant both the failure and the triumph, and move on to Schumpeter's rightful concern with the magnetic field between the three institutions.

Can democracy flourish without capitalism? Since no modern capitalist country seriously claims actual laissez-faire capitalism, by definition the question might just as well be: can democracy flourish without regulated capitalism? Nor need we be vague about defining democracy. At the very least, we mean representative government, where the knock on the door in the middle of the night is not heard, and where election winners with a taste for tyranny face ejection under the rule of law. For Schumpeter, democracy was important, but it had become basically a factional struggle for election among base contenders, whose winners then routinely governed the people, somewhat like political hacks.[14] This leaves little room for a moral vision of democracy, one of constantly expanding rights, and one able to resist economic, religious or other power at odds with popular sovereignty. The irony of Schumpeter's narrow vision is its failure to perceive how democracy and capitalism, as defined above, reinforce each other, enabling the institutions to flourish together. The very nature of bourgeois capitalism, with its fierce stake in free markets and free enterprise, creates a civil space against encroachment by an overreaching state, say a democracy losing its moorings. Conversely, the democratic state, enriched and enlightened by the broad-based education, health, literacy and taxes made possible by economic growth, can legislate the raw edges off capitalism by reforming its turbulent nature.

An additional phenomenon affecting this tense partnership has appeared in the so-called post-industrial society, possibly beyond Schumpeter's scope fifty years ago. In retrospect, centralized socialism, that is, state ownership of production accompanied by rigid state control of economic operations, appeared workable in the early days of heavy-industry industrialization. The Soviet Union not only demonstrated respectable war production in World War II, but its GNP, despite all the war-havoc and pre-war disruption caused by

123

forced collectivization, averaged approximately 5 per cent annual increase from 1955 to 1975.[15] The Russians were, and remain, the greatest oil producers other than the Saudi Arabians. The once thirteen million daily circulation of Pravda indicates a remarkable collaboration of technical efficiency with misinformation. The Soviets were also world-leaders in space exploration for years, although garrison-state comparative accomplishments should be ruled out for all contenders, including capitalist democracies. The point is, the Russian model failed gravely when faced with the high-tech production and maintenance demands of the second half of the twentieth century. The new 'information age' claimed as victims countries that suppressed information as official policy. It required complex, innovative technology and immediate response capability to maintain comparative productivity and economic growth. In this atmosphere, the new class of world-oriented, rational technicians typified by Gorbachev and to a lesser extent Yeltsin, realized they could not deliver an improved standard of living in peacetime under the secrecy and inefficiency of the centralized socialist structure. Ironically, the same rational, intellectual class that Schumpeter misread as disruptive in the future of American capitalism responded to Gorbachev's call for restructuring and openness by helping to overthrow Russian centralized socialism, compounding Schumpeter's faulty prediction.

There are, of course, other factors underlying the Russian collapse, notably the debased work ethic accompanying totalitarianism and the irrepressible instinct for personal freedom and ethnic identity. Concentration on Cold War armaments and imperialist adventures took their toll. Finally, the build-up of America as a superpower against the Soviet threat can be interpreted as a causal factor, if not an American victory, in the face of Russia's intransigence. In relation to capitalism itself, there is considerable reason to believe that the heavy hand of socialist economic control in the post-industrial period was far-outmatched by the market's invisible hand.

* * *

My preliminary answer to the question is, yes, democracy can flourish without capitalism, but at its own peril. After all, there is no

124

prescription for capitalism, other than the private property factor, in our founding documents. There may yet be a consensually-approved compound of democratic market-socialism somewhere in the future, along the Scandinavian path, still a 'middle-way' despite the 1991 ousting of Sweden's Socialist government. From a practical point of view, however, open-ended democracy, as we know it today, requires an alliance with capitalism, if the alternative is dominant centralized socialism.

For those wanting a record of the progress of triumphant democratic capitalism, Freedom House and similar sources show it to be firmly entrenched.[16] Indeed, a well-publicized analyst like Francis Fukuyama finds in democratic capitalism the end of western history's political journey, from Plato onward, subject only to adjustments. For more timely reassurance, the record shows that although capitalism has flourished without democracy, as in Franco's Spain and in the Pacific Rim's authoritarian economic successes, no modern democracy has survived without capitalism.

There we might let the matter stand, but the introduction of authoritarian examples causes us to consider the reverse of Schumpeter's prediction: what should one's response be to the march *away* from socialism? The encouraging news about authoritarian capitalism is the possibility – add Chile to Spain – of evolving into democratic capitalism. In South Korea, the education, literacy, middle-class affluence, and rational analysis generated by capitalism are expected in time to create a robust rather than repressed democracy. Even China, the remaining monolith of socialist legitimacy, now consciously runs the risk of democracy in its massive Guandong province market-economy experiment, in a population exceeding that of France. The vibrations from that area undoubtedly were heard in Tian An Men Square in 1989, but China's sophisticated rulers still call for more capitalist techniques and production, at the expense of socialist consistency. Possibly they fear economic stagnation more than capitalism and democracy. In each case, material benefits motivated the turn to capitalism. Since democracy and human rights do not appeal to authoritarian strongmen, our interests require democracy first, capitalism second.

Why, then, should America and its allies apparently make overnight free-market capitalism an implied condition for aiding Russia's march from socialism? Admittedly the range of foreign policy considerations, and the language involved, are too complex to discuss here, but surely the massive pain and inflation required by nationwide crash conversion can jeopardize the primary goal of exchanging democracy for dictatorship. Possibly the revival of neo-conservative economic ideology among American and European leaders, basking in the Russian débacle, has foreclosed the case for gradualism, with its concept that capitalism will follow democracy, the primary objective. It should be up to the almost-democratic Russians to decide if Gorbachev's inclination to use a portion of the old economic establishment rather than root it out is any sounder than Yeltsin's, or any successor's, reverse strategy. Certainly, the attainment of regulated capitalism in modern states has been a slow, give-and-take, evolutionary process, wherein relative stability generally follows restraining the free market from causing needless suffering and corruption. The case for contingent aid, unless it turns out to be flexible after all, is one requiring more debate in the donor countries.

* * *

Schumpeter's concern about capitalism, socialism, and democracy will carry on at a level of post-Cold War discourse beyond the 'burial of capitalism' and 'evil empire' stage. The laboratories for discussion will center on America, because of its democratic capitalist power, and China, because of its socialist solution for close to one-fifth of the world's population.

Understandably, there is not a word on China or Japan in Schumpeter's 1942 classic, illustrating the limits of predictability in a fast-moving century. Still respect should be paid for his intellectual courage. Without prophets and seers, there would be little room for moral vision in the human prospect. This limitation in Schumpeter's engagement with prophecy makes him less attractive for those interested in moral possibilities. Thomas Mann, in many ways Schumpeter's parallel in background and time, spoke eloquently for democracy from his exile in California while Schumpeter was at Harvard. Both were descendants of well-to-do capitalists.

126

Schumpeter's nostalgia for the entrepreneurs' archaic way of life pervades his work. Mann, in *Buddenbrooks* (1901), created a novel about the rise and fall of such a family, using the experience to ruminate on how institutions at their zenith contain the seeds of decay, infusing his work with a sense of change and fortitude.

2 Heilbroner's Vision

Robert Heilbroner, reviewing the recent biographies of Schumpeter, noted Schumpeter's repeated emphasis on the importance of 'vision' in the latter's valedictory *History of Economic Analysis*, namely, the intuitive framework controlling the subject's work sought by the historian-author. Applying such focus to Schumpeter's own generalizations, Heilbroner concludes that Schumpeter had unconsciously created an elitist social perspective that matched a desire to be recognized for his superior abilities.[17]

Heilbroner's own vision is based on a lifetime of analysis and reflection in the areas of economic history and systems. Identifying Heilbroner as a supporter of capitalism, although a cautious one, would constitute an important endorsement for the system. He could be seen as a representative of the intellectual class mediating for capitalism's survival.

We can examine Heilbroner's vision in terms of two concepts, first, the underlying nature and supporting apparatus behind the capitalist drive for profits, viewed largely from a Marxian perspective, and second, the present accommodation in which the 'two realms', democracy and capitalism, successfully coexist. The controlling vision is Heilbroner's consistent moral perspective.

Heilbroner has no illusions about the tyranny and distortion of idealism represented by Stalinist and similar regimes. He does not hesitate, however, to include his own understanding of Marxian analysis when it relates to his ongoing study. In analyzing the underlying nature of capitalism, he concludes that the pursuit of profit traces back to the basic drive for acquisition in the human personality. He finds that thinkers as varied as Smith, Marx, and Freud converge on the pursuit of prestige and power to satisfy this drive, formerly directed towards conquests and the raising of monuments by small ruling groups in the pre-capitalist age. Certainly prestige, or social recognition by others, is understandable as a strong motivation in modern social formations. Thorstein Veblen convinced a previous generation in that respect with his convoluted descriptions of conspicuous consumption. Power may not register so easily with those not by nature power-seekers. Here we can listen to the specialized Marxian argument for equating money with power, and power with domination, in a capitalist society.

* * *

The core focus of Marx's vision of the capitalist economic universe is power. We are accustomed to discussing power in relation to military and national ambitions, or in terms of religious and moral affairs, but to hear Marx, we must provisionally respond to the idea of capitalism as basically an exercise of economic power. Not the banal employer-employee relationships of everyday life, in which we speculate on the possibility of role-reversals, but in effect a world-view preoccupied with the injustice of employers secure behind their fortress of property ownership.

The new profit-motivated class, arising from the breakup of the feudal system, generated an economic process resembling a law of physics, or internal dynamics, resulting in the insatiable pursuit of more profits and more power. The formula for this perpetual profit machine is simple enough: $M - C - M'$. Money is converted into commodities ($M - C$). The commodities are of no use to the capitalists until converted once again into more money ($C - M'$). The process is then continually repeated. Above all, the new power base, controlling the forces of production, is able to treat labor as a commodity, extracting an unfair amount of the value added by labor in the inexorable process.[18]

A reductive summary of a portion of an immensely important analysis is a meagre introduction to Marx on profits, unlikely to generate either flames of revolt or agreement. Yet the Marxian preoccupation with power, profit, and control, however briefly presented, strikes home when we recall Chapter 4 herein, on capitalism and slavery. For over two hundred years in the eighteenth and nineteenth centuries, the British hegemony of capitalists, Parliamentarians, and clergy, all submitting to the insatiable urge for profits, collaborated in the collection and delivery of eight million Africans to New World plantation slavery.

* * *

A second Marxian claim is the subordination of the state to capitalism. Frequently quoted, the charge is made that the state acts as the executive committee for capitalism. We can dismiss this as hyperbole, as Heilbroner does, noting that in the capitalist-state relationship, only the primacy of capitalism, not its dictatorship, is warranted for reasonable observers.[19] A possible response, which Heilbroner finds operative, is to see such primacy as voluntary, a mutual but wary relationship between the two realms, based on need and practicality. The state reserves sovereignty, able to count on capitalist support in times of crisis or other showdown.

Nevertheless, even claims of primacy are serious and should be investigated. Non-Marxist analysts emphasize the pluralist nature of democratic capitalism, with interest boundaries rarely crossed, or at least subject to public outcry when blatantly violated, or limited by the Constitution, as in the case of church and state. For example, the sociologist Daniel Bell, in *The Cultural Contradictions of Capitalism* (1976), outlines three distinct realms in contemporary capitalist society, the economic, the political, and the cultural, each with its own nature and power. The discordances between the realms, though not fatal to the system, account for the cultural contradictions that concern Bell. Similarly, the moral philosopher Michael Walzer offers a strong defense of pluralism in *The Spheres of Justice* (1983). He is particularly concerned with crossovers at the boundaries, when the moneyed realm, for example, makes a bid to purchase power in the political realm, or when government seeks to control free inquiry in the educational realm, threatening democracy and its ideal of intellectual freedom.

It is Heilbroner's contribution to take a harder look at the equilibrium of pluralism, without diminishing the work of critics like Bell

129

and Walzer. Although he stresses the efficacy of the 'two realms', again the oversight is failure to recognize the pervasive effect of the nature of capitalism, the relentless drive to amass more profits that imposes rationalizing, cost-calculating restraints on government, and validates the commercialization of culture. If we find these forebodings less than threatening, offset by the welfare state, civil liberties, and cultural diversity, we must still recognize the presence of a genie requiring containment. Certainly an alliance of state, Congress and Court sanctioned the legalized repression of black citizens for a hundred years after their emancipation. True, democracy, and not capitalism, bears the burden of this inequity, but the vulnerability of the state to powerful interests speaks for itself.

* * *

The tense relation between the state and capitalism may become more problematical because of disruptions caused by the current model of world-capitalism, unapprehended by Marx. In this system, Heilbroner asserts, there is more at stake than the historic development of global, hegemonic networks of trade, finance, and raw materials exploitation that enabled core centers like Holland, England and America to dominate peripheral countries, as elaborated so well by Fernand Braudel and Immanuel Wallerstein.[20] Presently, national boundaries of all countries appear increasingly defenseless against elusive multinational corporations, including our own, ready to shift their production, research, and capital to the country with the best-trained work-force.[21] Equally disturbing, massive instant transfers of global money, seeking the best return, jeopardize national debt-financing and inhibit domestic policies seeking to restrain inflation and promote growth. The problem is aggravated by the rediscovery of economic power as the indispensable source of national political power, while grave ecological threats, such as global warming, require international cooperation.[22] It may be the defensive move to form world-class political and economic confederations is a first step toward meeting the next century's problems of global-capitalism. Heilbroner would welcome such a development, but sees little evidence of its imminent arrival.

130

A third feature of Marx on capitalism, the role of ideology as cynical instrument of support for the system, raises the prospect of possible thought-control. Participants in the free-wheeling intellectual atmosphere found in capitalist democracies find it difficult to accept the charge that values taught in schools, and disseminated by other institutions, are unreasonably loaded with supporting ideology.[23] Critics like J.K. Galbraith, who remonstrate us for adhering to the 'received traditions', are warmly greeted under the banner of intellectual freedom. An ideologue like Herbert Marcuse, claiming the existence of 'the one-dimensional man', so narcotized by capitalist creature comforts and the mass media that he does not realize he is half-formed, finds his audience. Heilbroner fully acknowledges the irony of the capitalist ambience that literally showers us with *lèse-capitale*, particularly in entertainment and on the campus.[24] Still he traces the reinforcing ideology in areas not overtly manipulative but questionable, such as the marketing of redundant goods, the commercialization of sports, and the debasement of culture. Again the nature of capitalism and its ideology are on trial. To what extent are Americans, regardless of party, conditioned to find values in 'private' concerns, but view 'public activity' with innate suspicion?

In discussing the Court and capitalism, we proposed the idea that the prevailing laissez-faire ideology of the elite sustained, if not explained, the Court's thirty-year rejection of most capitalist reforms. The reigning ideology, however, shifted with the times, following opinion changes among the elite and masses alike. In that sense, ideology continually creates its own dialectic. Though omnipresent in support of every regime, it appears not to qualify readily as cause or effect.

* * *

Can capitalism claim a friend in Heilbroner, castigated by Marxists and free-enterprisers alike for his relentless examination? We have noted and commented on his criticisms in the preceding section. Now for the positive side of his appraisal.

131

First, the alternative. Heilbroner maintains that centralized socialism, in which the state manages and controls all significant production, does not work. It is crucially flawed by authoritarian repression of information, resistance to change, and lack of incentives. Its tattered appeal remains largely in the claim that it is concerned with the moral, not just the material, elevation of mankind. In practical terms the question is whether centralized socialist economies can match the successful coexistence of democracy with capitalism, which also has moral potential, as this book claims. Heilbroner doubts whether the centralized state can yield enough authority to the economic realm to regain its standing as an efficient alternate to democratic capitalism.[25] Heilbroner is also concerned with the evidence that centralized states, authoritarian to start with, inhibit civil liberties, especially human rights, compared with democracies, eventually facing subversion on that basis. Capitalism, by nature open to change and innovation, adjusts well to the freedom element of democracy, reinforcing the latter's fundamental commitment to liberty and rights. It is true that capitalism favors property rights, but its great stake in free markets and free enterprise creates a formidable civil space that resists encroachment by the state, even a democracy running offcourse. Additionally, capitalism has accepted, not without struggle, a continual reduction in property rights, thereby achieving reasonable harmony on the democratic side.

Next, there is capitalism's favorable tilt towards cultural freedom, responding to the market's incessant demand for gratification and diversity. Here Heilbroner faces a dilemma. He sees no more merit in perpetuating the shoddy, life-devaluing aspects of capitalist culture than he sees in the market's deliberate environmental waste. Cultural waste, however, has no clear-cut alternative avoiding censorship or paternalism. Nevertheless Heilbroner would place it on the agenda as a matter for public concern.[26]

Another mixed review is granted to democracy's relationship with capitalism on the matter of social justice. The political realm, he notes, has the power to amend by vote the great differential in income and wealth existing in democratic capitalism. Much of the threat is diverted by the popular acceptance of inequality, shrewdly observed by Adam Smith as the tendency to admire rather than resent one's

132

superiors. Heilbroner concludes that a capitalist democracy will pursue welfarism on grounds of institutional adaptability, pragmatism, and fairness. No country has yet failed because of such expenditure. When the political realm seeks to increase entitlements, or indeed to increase the efficiency and growth of the economy itself, the economic realm ultimately concedes, recognizing the superior allegiance owed by the people to the state. Through such considerations, democratic capitalism has retained its vitality.

What of the future of democratic capitalism? For the near future, Heilbroner predicts an unexpected obstacle, global-capitalism, will upset the working accommodation established between the two realms. All nations, capitalist or socialist, face the interdependent effects of the coming world population explosion, the expansion of awesome technological frontiers, and the prospect of ecological doom.[27] In this context, even the most successful capitalist democracy will face a shift in its power balance toward the government rather than the economic system. External forces will thus affect the trajectory of capitalism's future, imposing restraints considerably beyond those now required to contain its internal drive for power. The preferred scenario would be for democratic capitalism to retain the best of its two realms.[28]

* * *

Heilbroner makes us think deeply about Schumpeter's triad of capitalism, socialism and democracy. Schumpeter, a sycophant of capitalism, abandoned the system even as it recovered from the Great Depression: the rules had changed; the game was no longer worth the candle. Heilbroner, a demanding critic, envisions possibilities in responsive democratic capitalism, qualifying as a friend.

Notes

1 Joseph A. Schumpeter, *Capitalism, Socialism and Democracy* (New York: Harper & Row, 3rd ed., 1950), 61.

2 *Ibid.*, 167.

3 *Ibid.*, 419.

4 Joseph A. Schumpeter, *The Theory of Economic Development* (Cambridge: Harvard University Press, 1934), 93–4.

5 See Richard Swedberg, *Schumpeter: A Biography* (Princeton: Princeton University Press, 1991); Also Robert Loring Allen, *Opening Doors: The Life and Work of Joseph Schumpeter* (New Brunswick: Transaction Publishers, 1991); also Richard P. Coe and Charles K. Wilber, ed., *Capitalism and Democracy: Schumpeter Revisited* (Notre Dame: University of Notre Dame Press, 1985); also *Journal of Democracy*, July 1992, Vol. 3,3.

6 Swedberg, *Schumpeter: A Biography*, 3.

7 Peter L. Berger, 'The Uncertain Triumph of Democratic Capitalism', *Journal of Democracy*, July 1992, 7–8. For those seeking a justification of capitalism from a conservative point of view, much admired by his liberal peers, see Berger's *The Capitalist Revolution* (New York: Basic Books, 1986).

8 Qu. by Jagdish Bhagwati, 'Democracy and Development', *Journal of Democracy*, July 1992, 37–8.

9 Robert Heilbroner, *The Worldly Philosophers* (New York: Simon and Schuster, 1953), 302–5.

10 *Ibid.*, 302.

11 Schumpeter, *Capitalism, Socialism and Democracy*, 381.

12 *Ibid.*, 158–60.

13 *Ibid.*, 138.

14 *Ibid.*, 282–83.

15 Ed Hewett, *Reforming the Soviet Economy: Equality versus Efficiency* (Washington, D.C.: Brookings Institution, 1988), 38.

16 Freedom House, founded in 1942 by Wendell L. Willkie, Eleanor Roosevelt and others, reports 99 'free' (the highest rating) nations in 1992, compared with 44 in 1972. It has announced a new agenda to influence U.S. foreign policy towards human rights, succeeding the old containment policy as the road to freedom. The policy is not burdened with free-market

134

conditions, unlike World Bank, CECE, and International Monetary Fund Policy pronouncements, often contradicted by their leading research experts.

17 Robert Heilbroner, 'His Secret Life', *New York Review of Books*, 14 May 1992, 31.

18 Heilbroner, *The Nature and Logic of Capitalism*, 36–52. Also see *supra*, Chapter 1, n.8.

19 *Ibid.*, 95.

20 See Fernand Braudel, *Civilization and Capitalism, 15th–18th Century* (New York: Harper and Row, 1981–84). In this three-volume work, Braudel first describes daily material life, then moves on to exchange markets. At the top of the economic structure, he locates capitalism as a multinational system controlled by bankers and major traders. As Heilbroner points out, (*Nature and Logic*, 35–6), Braudel shows little, if any, interest in the Marxian attribution of unique production and social powers for capitalism, although portraying successive eras of economic domination and unequal exchange. Immanuel Wallerstein, indebted to Braudel, has developed an in-depth school devoted to the concept of a world-economy wherein a series of core centers progress at the expense of peripheral members. The core center represents a ruling economic class, confident of its mission as same, though not intentionally domineering or exploitative. See *The Modern World-System* (New York: Academic Press, I, 1976; II, 1980).

21 Robert B. Reich, *The Work of Nations* (New York: Alfred A. Knopf, 1991), 243–51.

22 See Heilbroner's review of Paul Kennedy's *Preparing for the Twenty-First Century* (New York: Random House, 1993), in *The New York Times*, 14 February 1993. He agrees with Kennedy's detailed recital of the next century's fearsome realities, but asserts the response must be more aggressive, including re-assessing the 'imperatives of capitalism' as part of the global problem.

23 See Samuel Bowles and Herbert Gintis, *Schooling in Capitalist America* (New York: Basic Books, 1976). Bowles consistently denies the case for capitalism's reform. He argues against those who seek distributive justice within democratic capitalism with the same vehemence reserved for those on the far right.

24 Heilbroner, *Nature and Logic*, 138–39.

25 Robert Heilbroner, 'Reflections: The Triumph of Capitalism', *The New Yorker Magazine*, 23 January 1989, 98–109.

26 Heilbroner, *Nature and Logic*, 116–18.

27 *Ibid.*, 199–208.

28 See Robert Heilbroner, *21st Century Capitalism* (New York: W.W. Norton & Company, 1993), 121–62, in which Heilbroner maintains a cautious advisory stance towards capitalism. For the foreseeable, problem-plagued future, he advocates one should make capitalism work as well as possible as long as possible. Acknowledging capitalism as the agent of progress, Heilbroner warns against subordinating politically-just goals to economic achievements.

8 A moral measurement for capitalism

1 The Path of this Book

There is the assumption in this book that laissez-faire capitalism has
seen its day in America, and should be retired with gratitude for its
accomplishments in earlier centuries. Also, while benign capitalists
are all to the good, and should be well-rewarded, the three branches of
government, and the mediating institutions of press, church and the
intellectual establishment, are indispensable moderators for such a
powerful system.

Historically, the major reforms imposed on business institutions in
the twentieth century concentrated on restricting the raw power of
capitalism, the first economic system to enjoy relative autonomy from
the reigning political system. Moral measurement has not been a
major factor in establishing the power equilibrium between the state
and modern capitalism. As ultimate countervailing authority, the state
entered the regulatory arena reluctantly, largely because of the breakdown of the economy during the Great Depression. Capitalism, by
nature preoccupied with profits, has neither Utopian nor moral ambitions. Its legitimacy has rested on unprecedented material deliveries in
peace and war, and a hard-earned, tense compatibility with democracy. Democracy has been preoccupied with securing the negative
civil rights related to political abuse. It is now time to propose positive economic rights for democracy's intractable, least-advantaged
citizens. Here is where the moral measurement for capitalism should
start. The new criteria for rights to be proposed in this chapter are first,
more fairness in distribution of economic resources; and second, the

dignity and security arising from the ability to work gainfully during one's lifetime work span.

In reaching the moral measurement stage, we by-passed narrating the evolution of economic systems. There are ample histories and commentaries tracing the path of production and consumption from the command economies of Pharaohs and emperors, through the unitary medieval society, on to the rise of the merchant class, with its economic-warfare, mercantilist variation of capitalism, and then earth-shaking industrial capitalism itself. In these stages of transition, moral arbiters are given short shrift, other than in the Church-dominated, pre-modern period. Its just prices, interest prohibitions, and disdain for merchants gave such authority a bad image in the mind-sets of the new, breakaway power group. Rational calculators content with the restraints of civil and contract law, modern-age merchants rejected moral meddlers. The famed Protestant ethic, acclaimed for its marriage of gain with godliness, can also be seen as a tactical maneuver on the part of the worldly merchants. In America, the separation of church and state further distanced morality from the marketplace. All in all, a risky background for advocating a moral measurement for capitalism. Fairness is a better arbiter.

* * *

At the outset, we presented Judge Posner's wealth-maximizing model. It is one of the few theoretical constructs in the tradition of capitalism as a just enterprise, including that of Adam Smith, who found morality compatible with his innovative market system. Judge Posner prescribes the use of economic analysis for making choices as an effective moral constraint on capitalism. His procedure would not only maximize wealth for all concerned by maximizing efficiency, but would also bestow the moral sanction of consent. The consent factor, Posner asserts, is achieved when free bargainers trade off costs versus benefits to conclude their economic transactions, with the bargaining scale so limited that no one loses ground. Some may object that such implied consent is too far removed from substantive concepts of morality, such as right or wrong, just or unjust, to qualify for its mission. In reviewing the Court and capitalism, we noted Justice

138

Holmes' disdain for the notion that Lochner's bakery employees were in fact freely negotiating and thus consenting to the hours of their work week. Still, attention should be paid to Judge Posner's admittedly speculative economic analysis, which has gained marked success in the field of legal decision-making. Consent, after all, is basic to representative democracy, the political base of the most effective capitalist systems. In the shop of rights, many would choose consent over more material benefits. It is also the linchpin of Kant's moral philosophy of autonomy and contractual obligation, which Posner claims in support of his theory. Further, recognition of the theory's merits is a reminder to liberals that conservative voices must be heard, especially in view of the evidence that economic growth, a conservative talisman, is the road to less inequality. Finally, is there any doubt about the primacy of cost-efficiency for increasing social benefits under democratic capitalism? Its absence in our health-care system, compared with other advanced nations, is manifest.

* * *

In the virtue analogue, we placed on hold public morality, where capitalism can best be measured as an institution, to explore personal morality, the primary field of moral philosophy. A society is no better than its members, and how we live our lives should matter most.

Aristotle is the acknowledged connoisseur of virtue, having left in his lecture notes a mine of cataloging and commentary on the cardinal and subsidiary virtues. For Aristotle, the virtues are a means of indoctrinating moral behavior, enabling us to internalize good habits and dispositions. Guided by reason, the keystone of Greek philosophy, we can then make right, morally-based decisions. With the virtues incorporated in our way of life, Aristotle holds we can achieve the goal of a state of well-being, or flourishing. This concept has been the most durable western moral self-improvement paradigm, ingested by St. Thomas to supplement the Christian virtues of faith, hope, and charity (love). Aristotelian moral philosophy, updated, is enjoying a contemporary revival, notably in the communitarian movement, inspired by Aristotle's dedication to civic bonding, which communitarians see as an antidote to the alienation of modern individualism.

The Aristotelian perspective, earth-bound and realistic, is a favored point of departure for the moral philosophers cited in the analogue, who generally prefer a secular, moderately relativist platform for entry into ethical life, and reject the rigid, more absolute principles of the Platonic and Kantian traditions. Pragmatic and rational, the Aristotelian view can be recruited to support pluralist democracy and capitalism as well. More than competitive theories, it relates reasonably to the morally-reticent, results-oriented utilitarianism of Jeremy Bentham and John Stuart Mill, favored by modern liberal states and most contemporary social justice philosophers. We do well to make its acquaintance, aware that no sane politician will run on the Aristotelian or utilitarian tickets.

The analogue noted that the virtue concept has been historically corrupted, providing us with a bright-line warning concerning institutions. The example cited was the French Revolution, which converted the concept of multiple personal virtues into a single public virtue. The resultant 'republic of virtue' became a mask for an absolutist regime of terror. The lesson for capitalism is to draw a boundary limitation against any alliance with totalitarianism, economic or political. As Isaiah Berlin reminds us, how many lives have been sacrificed on the altars of Utopianism?[2]

* * *

The revolutionary government's trampling of liberty, equality, and fraternity is cited as an example of institutional moral failure. As an example of institutional success, plantation slavery, the most dismal moral aberration in our national memory, presents a startlingly ambiguous role for capitalism, first as accomplice in establishing slavery, and then as claimant for redemption through slavery's abolition. As accomplice, capitalism succeeded so well in the logistics of purchasing, financing, transporting, and breeding of slaves for profit that slave families comprised four million of America's thirty million population at the outbreak of the Civil War. The mother country's business in slavery was even more successful. The founding nation of capitalism not only imported most of the Southern states' slave-produced cotton for its Manchester looms, but also led the Continent in collecting and delivering ten million blacks from Africa, mainly to the Caribbean islands, Brazil and America, in the eighteenth and nineteenth centuries. Another institution, organized religion, distinguished itself in the immoral business. Sixteenth-century Iberian Catholicism participated militantly in the wholesale slaughter and enslavement of Amerindians under the banner of Christianizing the natives. In suit, the English church, save for its Quakers, performed as collaborators with capitalists and their Parliamentary sponsors until the abolitionist leaders brought all parties to their senses.

English Christianity eventually redeemed itself by leading the attack against the slave-trade and slavery itself, abolished by political action at the height of slavery's European profitability in 1833. A coincident claim for capitalism's redemption lies in the force of its antislavery free market-free labor ideology, as Adam Smith and ultimately the property-oriented Parliamentarians recognized. The dilemma of American slavery is symbolized by the anguish of Lincoln, who finally decided on moral principle against contending interests, mainly economic.

* * *

An analogue of unqualified institutional success in relation to the American experience is presented in the case of the Court and capitalism. The Court's reform of capitalism can be seen as an extension of the freedom metaphor, the liberation of labor from pervasive economic inequities. It also involves the problem of power, not only of capitalism but of government itself. Given authority over the other branches of government, the Court can become a tyranny, as Jefferson feared. The fact that the Court has maintained its august legitimacy indicates that its alternation of restraint and activism has worked in the long-run, although the time-lag exasperates partisans. Possibly the Court's approval-rating depends on the looming sovereignty of 'We the People', as much as on the appointment of wise and independent justices, as noted in Bruce Ackerman's argument. The Court's historic effect on capitalism has been to reform and refurbish it in preparation for the next century, when the Court will undoubtedly be asked to endorse further expansion of government's role in the economy. Such considerations concern the moral limitations of democratic capitalism. In the previous chapter, we reviewed Schumpeter's prediction that capitalism would march into socialism, comparing it with Heilbroner's vision of capitalism surviving, subject among other items to enlarging its moral boundaries.

2 The Role of Religion

The first part of Schumpeter's *Capitalism, Socialism and Democracy* is devoted to an even-handed analysis of Marx's theory of unconditional socialism. Answering his own question of how a mere theory could provoke such monumental results, Schumpeter states that Marxism must be seen as a secular religion, with all the inspirational and eschatological hopes residing in religion. In considering personal virtue, we noted that religion, our strongest and most ancient moral influence, is generally excluded from moral philosophy, probably because such philosophy originated as a pagan enterprise aimed at religious superstitions, and later was intellectually demolished by Enlightenment philosophic rationalism. Despite such charges, my own choice for fairness leads me to inclusion, particularly since the case has been made that not only democratic government restrains capitalism, but also that the mediating institutions of press, church, and the intellectual establishment are indispensable for its good conduct.

* * *

The press, incidentally, as the fourth branch of government is a secular guardian of democracy and capitalism, deserving special praise. We have noted its role in helping to overthrow slavery in England, as muckraker in attaining the economic reforms of the Progressive movement, and as interpreter between the Supreme Court and the sovereign people. An unlikely candidate for honorable mention in economic responsibility is the *Wall Street Journal*. Its 1.9 million circulation reaches the desks of practically every self-defined capitalist and power-elite aspirant in the country. Without scandal or sensationalism, it relentlessly records the crimes and chicanery of its subscribers and advertisers. Its daily revelations of securities fraud and corporate misdemeanors make us wonder what kind of sham capitalism existed before the New Deal. Many regard its editorials as from another planet, but surely the *Journal* reporters and guest columnists help keep capitalism in line.

* * *

Returning to religion as a mediating factor for economic justice, reaching institutionally beyond the area of personal conduct, note a strong voice is heard in the Catholic church. Certainly we must acknowledge the other major religions, each with vital traditions of social justice, stressing through their sermons and commissions on ethics corporate as well as personal responsibility.[3] We have noted the success of evangelical Christianity, following in the path of the Quakers, in terminating English slavery. The Protestant ethic survives in the workplace of capitalism, sanctifying efficiency. In an ecumenical sense, we can concentrate on the Catholic church, a segment of which has been particularly articulate on capitalism, as the analogue for religion.

This Church (capitalized for reference) has historically been antipathetic to business. At times it has been immorally associated with it, making its present distinction the more noteworthy. In discussing slavery, we related the fusion of faith, sword, and profits in the sixteenth-century conquest of the Amerindians. The revisionist judgment on that matter is the harsh reevaluation of Columbus upon the quincentennial of his epic voyage.

During the rise of capitalism in pre-Renaissance Europe, the Church was hostile to the emerging monied class. By nature totalitarian, its reach extended to all walks of life, including a doctrine of just, rather than market prices, as detailed in St. Thomas's *Summa*. Allied comfortably with the realms of monarchy and arms, the Church saw little need for a new estate of merchants, aside from fund-raising, notably for its Crusades. From this stance, the Church dispensed a steady flow of anti-trade ideology and sanctions. Moreover, like its major rival, Islam, the Church denounced all interest, not just a fair

143

amount, a frontal assault on the banking network essential for the growth of autonomous, large-scale trade. In a series of official Councils, peaking in the thirteenth century, usury was related to the sin of avarice and forbidden, subject to dire reprisals including excommunication.

This was hardly an environment for the birth of capitalism, a system now endorsed, with caution, by Pope John Paul II. As background, there is another side to Church economic history. First of all, the abandonment of trade to outsiders by both Church and state created an open space eagerly exploited by the profit-motivated, embryonic capitalists. The state, or its early equivalents, promoted business by maintaining distance from both the entrepreneurs and their ventures. Further development of capitalism, however, depended on state sponsorship, as protector on the seas, or of property rights in the courts, a matter often overlooked by economic libertarians. Similarly, the Church of the pre-capitalist period sponsored major advances in labor-saving technology, coincident with the introduction of thousands of water-mills throughout Europe. These manpower supplements were highly developed in the widespread monastic systems, whose abbeys employed large numbers of clerical and lay workers, efficient enough to find time for ample prayer and highly profitable production. This aspect of the aristocratic Church, consciously molded on the social structure of the vanished Roman Empire, was a turn away from the disdainful attitude towards work held by the Roman imperial elite, who chose not to use their great knowledge of water-power to lessen harsh toil. The monastic Church, inspired by Biblical injunctions to tame the earth and make it multiply, dignified common labor with the notion of *laborare est orare*, to work is to pray. Art historians confirm this change, comparing Jesus as emperor, seated on a Roman throne in the mosaics at Ravenna and St. Mark's in Venice, with Jesus as architect-engineer, bending over the earth with carpenter's compass in hand, in thirteenth-century illuminated manuscripts.

Indeed, the vicars on earth demonstrated immense capitalist talents in the age of cathedrals. I have remarked elsewhere how a man like Abbot Suger, presiding over the reconstruction of the abbey church of St. Denis, the prototype for the new, light-filled, soaring cathedrals, displayed formidable capitalist abilities as organizer, innovator, risk-taker, fund-raiser, even public relations expert in securing the aid of the Capetian kings, anxious to pursue their dynastic bid for a united France.[4]

On a broader scale, the durable Church, hierarchically structured yet delegating authority to strong, well-trained management, became a working example for the corporate world looming beyond the cathedrals. Ironically, the magnificent cathedrals were deficient in an essential capitalist requirement, that of economic feasibility. They could not have been built with any rational calculation of time or expense. In that respect, they serve to endorse the merit of a moral ingredient for capitalism.

* * *

What happened to the Church's ban on interest? Here the expedient side of the Church comes into play. At the upper level, both royalty and Church subscribed to a double-standard, paying willingly for the use of money. At a lower level, the crafty merchants invented a host of evasions, requiring borrowers to sign notes in excess of amounts received, or charging fees, premiums, or assignment of ownership shares to get their interest equivalents, much as Islamic banks do to this day. If all the usurers were banned by the Church as required by canon law, observed Innocent III in 1208, then all the churches might as well shut down. In effect, the Church's misguided moral effort amounted only to a hindrance, unable to prevent the rapid growth of trade and credit. The prohibition was rescinded in modern times, illustrating the Church's capacity to change slowly on all matters, including the recent absolving of Galileo's heliocentricism. A cautionary note for capitalism lies in the interest episode. The kings who borrowed recklessly from bankers showed no compunction in abrogating their debts, bringing ruin to the Bardi and other medieval banking houses who sought a share of political power as well as interest for their transactions. Capitalism is well-advised against embracing the state too closely, let alone attempting to dominate it.

3 The Archbishop as Mediator

Having reviewed the Church's experience in the capitalist arena, we introduce a current combatant, Archbishop Rembert Weakland, of the Milwaukee diocese. Weakland is known primarily for chairing the commission of the National Council of Catholic Bishops, which produced in 1986 the final version of an extraordinary pastoral letter on economic matters, as guide for Catholic teaching on the subject. Heroic figures of capitalism, not engaged in business itself, are rare enough, assuming they qualify as such in the first place. Two who have emerged in this book are Adam Smith, the first great expositor of a capitalist order, praised for his knowledge, style, and moral integrity, and Father Las Casas, the sixteenth-century priest who spent most of his lifetime campaigning against Spanish slavery in Central and South America, castigating it as an abuse of the profit system, often in the face of Charles V himself. Father Coughlin has been cast in a villain's role. It is difficult to realize how immensely popular he was, one-quarter of a nation reported as tuning in on his weekly call to abandon capitalism.

* * *

Rembert Weakland's career follows a favorite American tradition. The poorest of boys, nurtured by a strong, widowed mother, superbly educated and trained by a surrogate mother, the Church, becomes a world figure, tilts with the institution that fashioned him, and then makes his peace with the consequences.

He grew up in Patton, Pennsylvania, a remote coal-mining town in the Allegheny mountains. When he was six, his father, descendant of Catholic immigrants of pre-Colonial days, died in 1933, dejected over a fire that burned down the family-owned hotel a few years earlier. His mother, formerly a schoolteacher, now at home with six children, Rembert in the middle, had to go on relief, or public assistance as it was then termed. The future antagonist recalls years of meals based on powdered eggs, surplus corn meal, and milk allotted such families in the Roosevelt depression period.

The home possessed an upright piano. Largely self-taught, Rembert became a church organist while in the eighth grade. Although this talent tells more about aptitude than economic insight, it helped shape his destiny. The local pastor took a group of altar boys, including Rembert, to visit the Benedictine Archabbey of St. Vincent, sixty miles away in Latrobe. It was founded in 1846, the oldest Benedictine community in America, built in the austere Bavarian style, an inspiring, orderly complex of church, library, preparatory school, college, and monastery. Especially attractive were the numerous pianos and practice rooms.

When he was thirteen, his family sent him off to St. Vincent's Preparatory School, for a period of intense spiritual life, with time for lessons in Latin, Greek, and German, and endless hours at the piano and organ. In 1967, twenty-seven years later, at the Benedictine college of Sant'Anselmo in Rome, now his alma mater, the abbots from the world over met to select a new abbot primate. They settled on Rembert, then age forty and vigorous abbot of St. Vincent's, to head the world order, founded by Benedict of Nursia at Monte Cassino in the sixth century. This order, which dominated western monasticism from the sixth to twelfth centuries, made great contributions to education and economic development, while producing important Church leadership in that period. It exemplified the elevation of work, noted above as one of the seminal changes in the Catholic outlook. St. Benedict, himself a Roman aristocrat, scheduled at least six hours a day for constructive work, departing from the contemplative asceticism of the monastic convention. It is likely that this philosophic example, along with his precarious childhood, reinforced Rembert's emphasis on the basic right to work in his pastoral letter.

The Church had already sent him to Juilliard to study music for a year and then to Columbia to pursue PhD studies. As abbot primate, from his spacious quarters in Rome, Rembert reactivated the moribund office, visiting and restoring monasteries in Africa, Asia, South America, and behind the Iron Curtain, becoming a sophisticated cosmopolitan and linguist. In the process occurred the fateful event that would bring a monk, however eminent, into the select ranks of bishops, usually reserved for skilled theologians, philosophers, and canon experts. As a young musicologist researching Church music in Milan, he had become friendly with Archbishop Montini, who became

Paul VI in 1963 and subsequently appointed Weakland to the Milwaukee post in 1976. The binding force accounting for the elevation of both men was the influential papacy of John XXIII (1958–63), the aged former Archbishop of Venice, who rejuvenated Catholicism with his bold, unexpected Vatican II. This Council, finally promulgated in 1965, was a breakthrough call for change and modernization in the Church's structure and attitudes, ranging from condemnation of anti-Semitism to the replacement of Latin in ritual. Above all it called for recognition of man's entitlement to a life endowed with a sense of dignity and freedom of conscience, reflecting the input of the American theologian John Courtney Murray. High-level appointments were made in response to this call for activism, with approximately half of the present 300 American bishops appointed in the new tradition.

It is tempting to view the released energies of the bishops as an analogue of capitalist enterprise. Cyclically the corporate giants swing from over-centralized bureaucracy to massive decentralization, empowering middle-management to think and act for itself. The bishops reacted accordingly, proclaiming an unpopular, outspoken anti-nuclear statement in 1983, and engaging in liberation theology, or political intervention without regard for Marxian taint, particularly in Central and South America. As with the great corporations, headquarters in time feels it is losing control, and seeks to rein in the centrifugal force by changing personnel and rules. John Paul II, the present highly capable veteran of Cold War containment, has applied such restraints. A liberal activist concerning capitalism itself, John Paul II, faced with doctrinal subversion, has tightened command from Rome, an administrative decision which Weakland professes to understand, while acknowledging its chilling effect on his own career.[5]

* * *

The 1984 economic draft became a *cause célèbre* between politically conservative Catholic laymen and the liberal position of the bishops. The final 1986 edition, passed by a vote of 225 for, and 9 against, reflects little change. In essence, the letter declares the inequality of income and wealth in America morally unacceptable. It calls for government intervention to reduce this condition, giving a 'preferential option for the poor', and authorizing greatly increased funding for welfare programs, job-training, education, and health care, as well as Third World relief. It clearly supports the capitalist system, but in repetition of Vatican II, finds the free-market economy an anachronism. Adding salt to the wounds, the bishops assailed the cultural defects of contemporary capitalism: selfishness, consumerism, privilege, even avarice, the medieval deadly sin.

In June of 1984, an imposing group of dissenters, catching wind of the letter's contents, held a conference with Weakland, attempting to moderate its tone. In a scene worthy of a scriptwriter, Weakland recalls the parade of dark-windowed limousines to his door, and the entrance of eminent members of the lay Church. Headed by former Treasury Secretary William E. Simon and J. Peter Grace of W.R. Grace & Co., the group also included Michael Novak, scholar and theologian at the American Enterprise Institute. Novak's credentials as an articulate, vigorous champion of free-market capitalism are unquestioned. Indeed he is an eloquent advocate of the Church as a mediating influence on capitalism, providing it draws the line on unnecessary intervention by a government seeking redistribution rather than creation of wealth.[6] Still the idea of one intellectual, flanked by captains of industry, facing the lone bishop, is unsettling.

The confrontation needs context. The forthcoming presidential election would be fought largely on grounds of renewing Reagan's first term as triumphant free-enterpriser and de-regulator. The nation's 52 million Catholics, no longer a blue-collar, lower-income group, had helped produce the neo-conservative majority. Both parties recognized this conflict and agreed to release the draft only after the election. The Lay Commission, fortified by former Secretary of State Alexander M. Haig and Clare Boothe Luce, then mailed their views to 19,000 Catholic parishes, emphasizing their non-partisan belief in unencumbered capitalism as the road to social improvement. When the final version appeared in 1986, Weakland became a national figure, addressing a group of 400 Wall Street brokers and bankers, and the Joint Economic Committee of Congress. Government must intervene, he advised the Committee, to provide 'full employment... the foundation of a just economy.'[7] Soon he accused the Vatican of stifling dissent on religious matters, responding to the disciplining of

Archbishop Hunthausen of Seattle, and Father George Curran, moral theologian of Catholic University of America, calling on the spirit of Vatican II for support. By 1990, he knew he had reached too far. Invited to receive an honorary degree, his sixteenth, for the work on the economic letter from the University of Fribourg in Switzerland, he found the usual consent from Rome denied to the university. When a delegation from Fribourg flew to Rome to protest, they were advised his attitude towards pro-life groups, from whom he had requested more civility, lay behind the decision.

Meanwhile, on capitalism, John Paul II came through with flying colors. In a May 1991 major encyclical, 'Centesimus Annus', on the economic questions raised by the upheaval in Eastern Europe, he warned capitalist nations against letting the collapse of Communism blind them to the need to repair injustices at home. The free market, the encyclical declared, while the most efficient instrument for utilizing resources, does not meet human needs which find no place in the market. Capitalism must be circumscribed by a framework of laws and rights, it continued, as well as an ethical and religious understanding of human freedom. Archbishop Weakland stated: 'The Pope's approach to capitalism is exactly the one we took, to accept its good qualities but also to insist that it needs to be controlled and limited by other forces in society outside it.'[8] On August 27, 1991, William Simon and Michael Novak declared in the *National Catholic Reporter* that the Pope's encyclical endorsed a market economy and 'will do more to help the poor than any other encyclical.' Events since then have demonstrated that the bishops' letter helped restore to political and economic debate the neglected commitment to social justice.

4 The Case for Inequality: Rawls's Theory of Justice

We return to theory, after visiting the bishops and their politically-charged agenda, advocating more state intervention for capitalism at a time when liberalism was the banished 'L' word. In Chapter 1, we noted the prominence of John Rawls, a political philosopher with a theory of justice applicable to economic institutions, involving moral, or value, judgments about the distribution of social goods. The social justice branch of moral philosophy has limited membership. Most moral philosophers prefer to philosophize about personal ethics, how we, and not our institutions, should act in order to flourish. Also, they resist value judgments as being too subjective. Nor can we be sure about how much, if any, influence a theorist like Rawls can exert on government, the only area in which his principles can be converted into reality. Still, agenda alone will not suffice. Each agenda proposal, like restraints on capitalism in order to create full employment, generates passionate and often convincing counter-proposals, such as interference with growth, or fear of inflation. In reply, as with Lincoln and his contending interests over slavery, often only principle is left: large, prolonged unemployment, like slavery, is wrong. Alternately, we found the most attractive rhetorical principle, equality, transformed into terror in the French and Russian revolutions, cautioning us to maintain skepticism on such matters.

We have reiterated that capitalism, unlike socialism, has no moral blueprint, and this book has been a call to fill that void, without marching into Utopias. Ironically, capitalism has an effective principle in addition to free markets, that of inequality. The market system depends on unequal rewards and privileges, inherent in profits and competition. I have even suggested that capitalists, or upper-bracket earners as a class, gladly pay escalating taxes and accept the regulations of a welfare state as the price, or ransom, for such inequality and privilege. Rawls can be seen as an advocate of contingent inequality, certainly not of equality alone. Defenders of capitalism may well make his acquaintance, as we did with Aristotle, presented as pragmatic and experimental in the capitalist sense. Rawls does not specify a preferred economic system, but he advocates a property-owning regime as best-suited for his justice theory.[9]

As with the philosophers discussed earlier, Rawls sets out to demolish a rival moral and social theory, the reigning utilitarianism, vulnerable for its inability to accommodate personal preferences because of its value-free devotion to results or consequences. Rawls identifies his theory as contractarian, or Kantian. In that role, he describes a simulated voyage of highly objective, independent and selfless founders embarked, like similar covenanters in history and literature, in search of fair rules and priorities for their just new world. Their decisions are guided by a fine-tuning of rationalism with intuition, resulting in a balance of 'reflective equilibrium', at which point choices are made, with Kantian personal autonomy preserved as far as possible.

Selecting from his rigorous, highly-structured theory, we can proceed to Rawls's Difference Principle, which is the core of his concept of justice as fairness. Differentiation itself is an indication of inequality. Rawls is keenly aware of the inescapable differences allotted at birth. We may be born free, or equal, but environment, genes, gender, and material inheritances soon take over. Concerned with total public life, Rawls proposes his Difference Principle as the guiding criteria for political, economic, and social institutions. The criteria consist of two principles. Since they have undergone changes following their original appearance in 1971, below is the latest version (1982 Tanner Lectures):[10]

1 Each person has an equal right to a fully adequate scheme of equal basic liberties which is compatible with a similar scheme of liberties for all.
2 Social and economic inequalities are to satisfy two conditions. First, they must be attached to offices and positions open to all under conditions of fair equality; and second, they must be to the greatest benefit of the least advantaged members of society.

The first principle is political: equal liberty, without exception, for all. The second principle permits minimum inequality in social and economic matters.[11] It is the second principle that deals with the fair distribution of society's resources. The ambiguous 'offices and positions' is clarified by Rawls's explanation that it means the 'primary social goods' that reasonable people would want most: rights and liberties in the political area, and income and wealth, opportunities and powers, and, finally, a sense of one's own worth in the economic and social areas. In this respect, theory has converged with reality. Since 1971, equal opportunity has become mandatory in the workplace, although Rawls has a broader, life-enhancing vision in mind, and dignity through work-entitlement has become essential in the Catholic economic agenda, as noted.

How are we to allocate these distributions, assuming everyone in the theoretical construct starts evenly? Rawls's shift to inequality is limited by the Pareto-superiority scale we encountered in Chapter 1, enlisted by Judge Posner to keep his economic analysis theory in bounds and morally acceptable. No one can get more unless the least advantaged at the bottom gain some improvement. That this limitation is basically considered an efficiency device is no problem for Rawls, whose theory requires efficiency considerations at every step, again in the capitalist tradition. Rawls, of course, is not a capitalist apologist, his list of 'primary social goods' being directed towards flourishing far beyond the material level. Still he can be seen as an advocate of morally-expansive, rights-based, democratic capitalism. His First Principle is a call for broad negative rights restraining the state in the name of liberty, as in the Bill of Rights and Civil War amendments. His Second Principle specifies new, positive economic and social rights.

* * *

Every moral theory has its dialectic. A successor arises who appropriates the old theory, amends it to reflect his own concern, and gives us a deeper understanding of the original. Rawls's interpreter and improver is Amartya Sen, like Rawls preeminent in his field. Sen's *Inequality Reexamined* (1992) claims that the real issue is inequality, not equality. The rhetoric of equality can divert us from the fact that since we are so varied by nature and fortune, social evaluations have more to do with inequality and its rectification. Acknowledging his debt to Rawls's theory as the most influential and important modern theory of justice, Sen is particularly motivated by Rawls's primary good of opportunity. In effect, he converts Rawls's breakthrough concern for opportunity for the disadvantaged into a new primary good, capability. Without capability, or access to the goal of flourishing, the least advantaged may never progress.[12] Recall in Chapter 5, concerning the hypothetical Guaranteed Work Act, that those at the bottom considered their hard-won civil rights a hollow victory, since jobs were not available.

Sen maintains that Rawls's theory treats the primary goods as means, without adequate provision for achieving the goals they imply.

153

Focusing on capability relates to the real world's increasing awareness of inequality, and the roles of education, vocational training, health care, child care, and full employment in reducing inequality to a fair level.

5 A Moral Measurement for Capitalism

After a rain of agenda in the 1992 elections, following a prolonged dry spell, it may be a relief that no further agenda follows here. Moral measurement takes cover under abstract, general principles. It claims non-partisan status and avoids practical cost analysis. Moral measurement looks to victory in the long-run, when a majority of votes may go its way, whatever the actual historical reasons.

I propose two 'Principles of Fairness' for the continuing reform and moral justification of democratic capitalism.

1 Reduction of Poverty
The officially-defined poverty class must show a continual and substantial decline year after year, involving sufficient government intervention to implement this trend.

2 Guaranteed Work Act
Congress must pass a guaranteed work act for those willing and able to work. For welfare recipients, government programs must provide vocational training, child care, health care, and financial incentives, enabling recipients to join the guaranteed work force.

Reduction of Poverty

Official statistics about poverty are its best advocate for government intervention. Americans have information about the profile of poverty as never before. Only the existence of a large middle-class, with its 'culture of contentment' on this subject, has repressed the problem. The plight of the 'homeless', in large part pathologic and not economic, has further diverted attention from the structural trend of poverty.

Briefly, the official figures can be recapitulated.[13] In 1990, the total poverty count was 35.7 million, 14.2 per cent of the total population. Who are they? 23.6 per cent of all children in America under six live in poverty. What color for the total count? About 85 per cent white. Is there a long-term, intractable trend in evidence? 12 per cent total poverty in 1969 against the above 14.2 per cent in 1991, twenty-two years later. How many are on welfare? Approximately 11.6 million Americans are on welfare, the majority single parents with dependent children. The welfare increase since 1990 exceeds the sixteen-year increase from 1973 to 1989: if you are poor, it is now much harder to stay off welfare. Twenty-seven million Americans depend on federal food stamps to supplement their welfare or other income.

Anything worse to add? Yes, poverty is undermining our major cities, the nerve-centers and power terminals of any civilization, capitalist or socialist. Here at least the 'cultural contentment' factor is receding in the face of middle-class fear, but any motivation, moral or other, should be welcomed. The subculture of alienated, inner-city poor is mired in a decayed and jobless environment, fostering crime, drugs, health problems, violence, and *de facto* segregated schools at enormous cost to society, including national competitiveness. Practically all Americans can relate to a previous generation of inner-city poor, mostly emigrants, whose schools, churches, voluntary associations, and role models in a highly-diversified population, economic and otherwise, eased the path of upward mobility. The great loss of blue-collar manufacturing jobs, the educational barriers to new urban high-skilled jobs, and the massive flight to the suburbs have changed the odds, regardless of serious charges of personal irresponsibility and disintegrating family structure. Who, changing places, would not feel abandoned and stratified? Who, other than the federal government, can mount an integrated attack on the urban aspect of poverty? Granted, President Johnson's War on Poverty thirty years ago was ineffective; the problem is still with us.[14] As a matter of principle, both capitalism and democracy require a permanent, national assault on poverty, with no scorecard of victory other than year-to-year substantial reduction, as with the annual budget deficit.

155

Such an act, hopefully passed in times of relative prosperity, would admittedly mark the departure of those who view it as one step too far in the progress of regulated capitalism. Short of government ownership of production far beyond the present scope, a guaranteed work act could be seen, with reason, as provoking apprehension far beyond the exaggerated fears of the 1937' Wagner Act, guaranteeing collective bargaining for unions.

The concern, aside from rhetoric about the end of capitalism, would center on two points, the cost in efficiency and the cost in dollars. As the principle indicates, the act would be least controversial in the area relating to welfare reform, where it could first be launched. Workfare is now a bipartisan concept, the long-term result of Senator Moynihan's courageous measurement of the welfare population and its dynamics in the 1960s. Workfare is already being tested at the state level. The cry of 'forced labor' holds little support since generous exclusions and support systems are inevitable. The missing factor is government as employer of last resort, even in times of full employment. Workfare, without appropriate work designed for welfare recipients, won't work.

There is no need for details for the Second Principle, other than the general outline in the hypothetical Guaranteed Work Act approved by the Supreme Court at the opening of Chapter 5. The Court was not concerned with efficiency or cost, leaving those matters to the Congress and its tax-paying constituents. The latter believed long-run, double-digit unemployment itself imposed a cost factor on industry impeding efficiency. Additionally, the new efficiency model was an educated, innovative work force, able to get its share of high-profit components in the new global-capitalism which in turn would determine a country's ongoing standard of living. As for cost, it was demonstrated that the new payrolls, mostly at entry level or less, thus reducing inflationary pressures, flowed back almost entirely in income taxes and consumer purchases, as with Social Security payments. The offsetting savings in unemployment and disability taxes for industry, and welfare costs for government, further mitigated the change.

Guaranteed employment is a benefit whose time has come, as surely as the advent of guaranteed health insurance for the entire nation. It will be delayed by budget problems and unexpected global events. Typically America has followed rather than led other capitalist nations in economic rights, but eventually one nation follows the other, levelling the competitive costs. Article 1 of the constitution of the New Germany states: 'The dignity of man shall be inviolable.' Dignity and citizenship mean inclusion in the workplace: what you are becomes more and more what you do. It is a worthy principle for the ongoing reform of democratic capitalism.[15]

This book has intended to raise our moral vision of capitalism by viewing it from unexpected promontories: contending versions of moral and political philosophy, analogues of virtue, slavery, and constitutional law, speculation on the future of democratic capitalism, the place of intermediating institutions, and, finally, a new set of principles. It has stressed that intervening government is the indispensable partner and guardian of capitalism, an economic system which should not only be valued but evaluated.

Notes

1 See *supra*, Introduction, n.1.

2 Isaiah Berlin, *Four Essays on Liberty*, (London: Oxford University Press, 1969), 118–72.

3 A contrary note concerning religion as a mediating influence on capitalism can be observed in the case of Japan, the new capitalist dynamo. Widespread religious skepticism followed the desacralization of the Emperor. Buddhism and Shinto, the leading religions, have no supererogatory authority in the Western religious sense. Japanese self-reliant morality seems no hindrance to capitalist performance.

4 Michelman, *The Roots of Capitalism in Western Civilization*, 157–61.

5 Paul Wilkes, 'The Education of an Archbishop', *The New Yorker*, 15 July 1991, 57–8.

6 Michael Novak, 'Changing the Paradigms: The Cultural Deficiencies of Capitalism', in *Democracy and Mediating Structures*, Michael Novak, ed. (Washington, D.C.: American Enterprise Institute, 1980), 180–210. There

is no mention of Archbishop Weakland in Michael Novak, *The Catholic Ethic and the Spirit of Capitalism*, (New York: The Free Press, 1993).

7 Wilkes, 'The Education of an Archbishop', 51.

8 *New York Times*, 3 May 1991, A-10.

9 John Rawls, *A Theory of Justice*, (Cambridge: Harvard University Press, 1971), 265–74.

10 Reprinted in John Rawls, 'The Idea of an Overlapping Consensus', *Oxford Journal of Legal Studies*, 1987, 5. The principles remain essentially unchanged in John Rawls, *Political Liberalism* (New York: Columbia University Press, 1993), 291. The aim of the new book is to address fairness in political matters in a society of competing beliefs, rather than the 'well-ordered' society of consensus assumed in *A Theory of Justice*. No particular attention is paid to economic distribution in the new book, and a narrow concept of property rights is reaffirmed, 297–98.

11 A special ordering, applicable to Rawls's Difference Principle, stipulates that political liberty ranks prior to social and economic choices, should choice be necessary. See *A Theory of Justice*, 43.

12 Amartya Sen, *Inequality Reexamined*, (Cambridge: Harvard University Press, 1992), 86–7. Also see *supra*, Chapter 2, n.7.

13 Sources: Economic Report of the President, 1987 and 1992; Children's Defense Fund, *The State of America's Children 1991*; U.S. Bureau of the Census; Statistical Abstract 1989, Table 604. The present officially-defined poverty level for a family of four, excluding non-cash benefits, is $14,350. It is based on three times food expenses calculated by the Agriculture Department, and a survey of about 60,000 households by the Census Bureau.

14 For a provocative, highly-publicized attack on government intervention against poverty, see Charles Murray, *Losing Ground* (New York: Basic Books, 1984). Murray charges that government programs produced more poor than more for the poor, and rather than providing an escape, built a trap. As a partial response, Albert O. Hirschman cautions us to see this type of broad conclusion as a 'thesis of perverse effect', consistently used against reform measures. See Albert O. Hirschman, 'Reactionary Rhetoric', *The Atlantic Monthly*, May 1989. For a balanced, item-by-item response, see Christopher Jencks, *Rethinking Social Policy* (Cambridge: Harvard University Press, 1992), 70–91. Jencks credits Murray with

casting the problem not on cost, or partisan revisions of cost, but on whether it works. Jencks claims the War on Poverty worked, but also rewarded irresponsibility. He supports reasonable workfare.

15 For a compelling argument for the right to work, see Judith N. Shklar, *American Citizenship: The Quest for Inclusion*, (Cambridge: Harvard University Press, 1991), 63–104. Shklar avoids moral claims, stating a right to earned work is as fundamental to American citizenship as the right to vote. She emphasizes the psychological and social loss related to involuntary unemployment. On the constitutional issue, see Frank Michelman, 'Welfare Rights and Constitutional Democracy', *Washington University Law Quarterly* (Summer 1979), concerning a social minimum for basic needs.

Index

161

167

168